ITIL® 4 High-velocity IT (HVIT)

Your companion to the ITIL 4 Managing Professional HVIT certification

ITIL® 4 High-velocity IT (HVIT)

Your companion to the ITIL 4 Managing Professional HVIT certification

CLAIRE AGUTTER

IT Governance Publishing

Every possible effort has been made to ensure that the information contained in this book is accurate at the time of going to press, and the publisher and the author cannot accept responsibility for any errors or omissions, however caused. Any opinions expressed in this book are those of the author, not the publisher. Websites identified are for reference only, not endorsement, and any website visits are at the reader's own risk. No responsibility for loss or damage occasioned to any person acting, or refraining from action, as a result of the material in this publication can be accepted by the publisher or the author.

ITIL® is a registered trade mark of AXELOS Limited. All rights reserved.

Apart from any fair dealing for the purposes of research or private study, or criticism or review, as permitted under the Copyright, Designs and Patents Act 1988, this publication may only be reproduced, stored or transmitted, in any form, or by any means, with the prior permission in writing of the publisher or, in the case of reprographic reproduction, in accordance with the terms of licences issued by the Copyright Licensing Agency. Enquiries concerning reproduction outside those terms should be sent to the publisher at the following address:

IT Governance Publishing Ltd
Unit 3, Clive Court
Bartholomew's Walk
Cambridgeshire Business Park
Ely, Cambridgeshire
CB7 4EA
United Kingdom
www.itgovernancepublishing.co.uk

© Claire Agutter 2021

The author has asserted the rights of the author under the Copyright, Designs and Patents Act, 1988, to be identified as the author of this work.

First edition published in the United Kingdom in 2021 by IT Governance Publishing.

ISBN 978-1-78778-295-2

ABOUT THE AUTHOR

Claire Agutter is a service management trainer, consultant and author. In 2020, she was one of Computer Weekly's Top 50 Most Influential Women in Tech. In 2020 and 2021, she was recognised as an HDI Top 25 Thought Leader and was part of the team that won itSMF UK's 2017 Thought Leadership Award. Claire provides regular, free content to the IT service management (ITSM) community as the host of the popular ITSM Crowd hangouts, and is the chief architect for VeriSM™, the service management approach for the digital age. Claire is the director of ITSM Zone, which provides online IT service management training, and Scopism. She has worked with ITGP to publish *Service Integration and Management (SIAM™) Foundation Body of Knowledge (BoK), Second edition* and *Service Integration and Management (SIAM™) Professional Body of Knowledge (BoK), Second edition*, the official guides for the EXIN SIAM™ Foundation and Professional certifications.

After providing support to thousands of people taking ITIL training and certification from version 2 onwards, she has created this series of books for those studying towards ITIL 4 Managing Professional and Strategic Leader status.

For more information, please visit:
- *https://itsm.zone*
- *www.scopism.com*

Contact:
- *www.linkedin.com/in/claireagutter/*

About the author

- *https://twitter.com/ClaireAgutter*

To learn more about Claire's other publications with ITGP, visit:

www.itgovernancepublishing.co.uk/author/claire-agutter.

CONTENTS

Introduction 1
   How to use this book 1
Chapter 1: Introduction to High-velocity IT 5
   High-velocity IT key terms 5
   When to transform 13
   High-velocity IT objectives 15
Chapter 2: The digital product lifecycle and the ITIL operating model 19
   The four dimensions of service management 19
   The VUCA environment 22
   The digital product lifecycle 23
   The service value system 25
   The service value chain 29
   Service consumer 34
   Value streams 36
Chapter 3: HVIT key behaviours 41
   Behaviour 1: Accept ambiguity and uncertainty 43
   Behaviour 2: Trust and be trusted 44
   Behaviour 3: Continually raise the bar 44
   Behaviour 4: Help to get customers' jobs done 44
   Behaviour 5: Commit to continual learning 44
Chapter 4: Principles, models and concepts 47
   Ethics 48
   Safety culture 49
   Lean culture 51
   Toyota Kata 55
   Lean/Agile/resilient/continuous 56
   Service-dominant logic 58
   Design thinking 59
   Complexity thinking 60

Contents

Chapter 5: Ensuring valuable investments 65
   Techniques for ensuring valuable investments 65
   Using the ITIL 4 practice guides....................................83
   ITIL practices and ensuring valuable investments.........83
Chapter 6: Ensuring fast development 95
   Techniques for ensuring fast development.....................95
   ITIL practices and ensuring fast development 137
Chapter 7: Ensuring resilient operations 165
   Techniques for ensuring resilient operations 165
   ITIL practices and ensuring resilient operations 202
Chapter 8: Ensuring co-created value 231
   Techniques for co-creating value 231
   ITIL practices and ensuring co-created value 236
Chapter 9: Ensuring assured conformance.................245
   Techniques for ensuring assured conformance............245
   ITIL practices and ensuring assured conformance.......259
Chapter 10: Exam preparation.....................................271
Appendix A: Banksbest case study................................275
   Company overview 275
   Company structure 276
   Future plans 277
   IT services 277
   IT department 278
   IT service management 279
   Sample employee biographies......................................279
Further reading..281

INTRODUCTION

How to use this book

The majority of this book is based on the ITIL 4 High-velocity IT (HVIT) publication and the associated ITIL 4 Specialist High-velocity IT syllabus.

In addition to helping you prepare for your certification, I also want to give you some advice and guidance that will lead to you using this book once your training and exam are over. I've added some of my own practical experience to this book and given you some advice and some points to think about along the way. My goal is for you to refer back to this book in years to come, not just put it away once you've passed your exam. With this additional content, you'll find this book is an excellent supplement to any training course and a useful tool in your ongoing career.

As you read the book, assume that all the content is related to the ITIL 4 Specialist High-velocity IT syllabus unless it is highlighted in one of two ways:

Introduction

Something for you: a small exercise for you to complete to apply the ITIL 4 concepts in your own role, or a point for you to think about. This content is not examinable.

Practical experiences: any content marked with this image is based on my own experience and is not examinable.

The content highlighted as something for you to think about or practical experience might also refer to the Banksbest case study you can find in Appendix A. I'll use the case study to give an example of how something would work in the real world, or to help you apply what you're reading about. Case studies can really help to bring abstract concepts to life. The case study is not examinable, but using it will help you get a deeper understanding of the HVIT concepts you are learning.

Let's start with something for you now:

Introduction

Why not read the case study and make a note of your first impressions of the Banksbest organisation and its plans before you study the HVIT content in this book?

Unless stated otherwise, all quotations are from *ITIL® 4 High-velocity IT* and *Practice Guides* published by AXELOS in 2020. Copyright © AXELOS Limited 2020. Used under permission of AXELOS Limited. All rights reserved.

CHAPTER 1: INTRODUCTION TO HIGH-VELOCITY IT

In this chapter, we introduce High-velocity information technology (HVIT). The topics in this chapter include:

- HVIT key terms;
- When the transformation to HVIT is desirable and feasible; and
- The five HVIT objectives.

The ITIL 4 HVIT publication *"aims to help readers understand digital transformation and to guide them and their organizations towards a more integrated state between business and technology. By discussing organizational best practice and useful mental models from a practitioner's perspective, it provides invaluable guidance in the practical application of high-velocity IT."*

High-velocity IT key terms

The key terms that you need to understand for HVIT are:

- Digital organisation
- High-velocity IT
- Digital transformation
- IT transformation
- Digital products
- Digital technology

1: Introduction to High-velocity IT

Digital organisations

A digital organisation is one *"that is enabled by digital technology to do business significantly differently or do significantly different business"*.

For these organisations, digital technology is:

- A significant enabler for internal processes;
- Often part of their products and services;
- A strategic part of the business model; and
- For primary activities, not just supporting activities.

Digital organisations may also be described as 'digitally enabled'. Their culture is 'digital first'.

Think about the concept of a digital organisation. Which companies come to your mind first? You might think of organisations like Uber, Apple or Airbnb. These organisations have all had digital technology embedded in their business model from the beginning, but can you also think of any organisations that have changed how they do business because of technology? For example, a magazine or newspaper that has moved to an online version rather than printed copies.

When we think about digital organisations and HVIT, we need to remember the organisations that will change because of technology, not just organisations that have embraced technology since their inception. Organisations

1: Introduction to High-velocity IT

> that change how they do business will face bigger challenges as they try to change their strategy and their culture, but they will also have the potential to gain huge rewards.

High-velocity IT

"High-velocity IT is the application of digital technology for significant business enablement, where time to market, time to customer, time to change, and speed in general are crucial. It is not restricted to fast development; - it is required throughout the service value chain, from innovation at the start, through development and operations, to the actual realization of value."

Velocity encompasses speed and direction – do the right things, quickly. Increasing velocity has costs and risks, and each organisation must assess whether a High-velocity approach will deliver a return for them.

> Have you heard this project management expression? "A project can be good, fast or cheap. Pick any two from that list, because you can't have all three!"
>
> The idea of a project that was good, fast AND cheap was seen as impossible. In my experience, this was true for many projects that I worked on. Picking the cheapest

1: Introduction to High-velocity IT

quote often led to a poor-quality outcome, or a tight deadline could only be achieved for a higher price.

Is this still the case? I'd argue that it is not. There are some significant shifts in IT and business thinking that mean that we can frame this problem in a different way.

First, the shift from waterfall projects to more agile ways of working means that we look at both 'good' and 'fast' differently. If we are working iteratively, we have a series of short, predictable deadlines rather than one goal to aim for. 'Good' is an outcome that is achieved over multiple iterations. The first idea or demo might not be 'good', but the feedback that it creates helps to deliver a better end product.

The shift from project to product thinking (and teams structured in the same way) also changes this equation. A product might never be complete; instead, it is continually refined. And finally, evidence[1] shows that organisations that make more changes (move 'fast') get better at making changes and deliver more value.

HVIT encompasses many of these ideas. Speed is good, but remember that it's a means to an end. Speed for speed's sake isn't the goal. Speed to increase our ability to deliver better outcomes is our ultimate aim. Speed must work within the context of our organisation and any constraints that apply to our business.

---

[1] *https://cloud.google.com/blog/products/devops-sre/the-2019-accelerate-state-of-devops-elite-performance-productivity-and-scaling*.

1: Introduction to High-velocity IT

Digital transformation

"Digital transformation is the use of digital technology to enable a significant improvement in the realization of an organisation's objectives that could not have been feasibly achieved by non-digital means."

IT transformation

"Where business and IT are regarded as separate organisational functions, 'IT transformation' can be used to denote major change to improve how IT services are provided."

'IT transformation' includes how IT systems and services are developed, run and supported. If the business and IT are not viewed as separate entities, there is no distinction between IT transformation and digital transformation.

Be careful with the concept of 'IT transformation'. In many organisations that I've worked with, the IT department operates as a separate entity, distinct from 'the business'. This is a source of cultural issues, can stifle innovation, and leads to the rise of 'shadow IT' (defined as IT solutions procured without the authority or oversight of the IT department). If we accept that digital transformation puts technology at the heart of most (if not all) of our business processes, the idea of IT running its

1: Introduction to High-velocity IT

own fiefdom immediately suggests a silo, along with all the problems that creates.

'Digital transformation' is also problematic as a term. Transformation means a process of change, with an implied start date and end date. This has led to the rise of 'digital transformation' projects, consultancy initiatives, organisational change programmes, etc. Think instead of digital transformation as being a thread that will always run through your organisation and its activities. It's not a single big change from state A to state B; rather, it is a constant assessment of how technology can improve ways of working and add value. Look at it another way – you don't hear companies talking about an 'automation transformation' where they spend 18 months automating things and then never look at automation again.

Nevertheless, digital transformation is the accepted and most popular term (try an online search!), so we are stuck with it. Just make sure you think critically about it and don't get sucked into large flashy programmes. Iterative, incremental changes will always be more effective.

Take a look at the Banksbest case study and see what you can learn about the organisation's digital transformation efforts. What positive changes do you see? Are there any red flags or warning signs that you would make Banksbest aware of if you were advising them? For example – how

1: Introduction to High-velocity IT

> do you feel about the CIO and CDO roles? Is it helpful to separate them or not?

Digital products

"A product is a configuration of an organisation's resources designed to offer value for a consumer. A product is digital when digital technology plays a significant role in its goods, resources, or associated service interactions."

Products could include mobile phones, software, websites, cars, etc.

Some products have both digital and physical elements; for example, your car might be delivered with an app to tell you where it is parked.

Remember from your ITIL 4 Foundation course that a service offering between a consumer and a provider can be one or a combination of three elements:

- **Service action:** *"A service action is where the service provider applies its resources."*
- **Access to resources:** *"When the consumer utilizes the provider's resources."*
- **Transfer of goods:** *"When the consumer acquires ownership of the service provider's resources."*

1: Introduction to High-velocity IT

What digital products did you use today? Did they save you time or money, or allow you to accomplish something you couldn't have done without access to technology?

Digital technology

"Digital technology is technology that digitizes something or processes digital data."

"Digitization is the process of transforming something from analogue form to digital form, by expressing the information in binary digits."

Digital technology includes information technology and parts of operational technology that have been digitised.

From an ITIL 4 perspective, information technology is *"the application of digital technology to store, retrieve, transmit, and manipulate data (data processing), often in the context of a business or other kind of organisation"*. Operational technology is *"the application of digital technology for detecting or causing changes in physical devices through monitoring and/or control"*.

1: Introduction to High-velocity IT

Very early in my career, I worked with an organisation where staff would print out 'important' emails so they could guarantee access to them if the system failed. When I started my role at the organisation, we had capacity issues relating to the filing cabinets stuffed full of printouts. When I left the organisation, we had virtual capacity issues due to digital hoarding instead (remember, this was at a time when storage was local and expensive).

The use of information technology has led to huge benefits, but with research showing that data centres and technologies like Bitcoin are having a significant negative environmental impact, our governance and our policies are just as important as the technology we use. This is where service management thinking can add real value. Technology will always be used by humans, and, as humans, our behaviour doesn't always make sense. Operational technology, for example, can give us amazing insights into potential failures, or it can lead to our on-call teams being woken at 2:00 am with irrelevant messages.

From a HVIT perspective, we have to keep our focus on the value that technology can deliver, and not get distracted by the latest shiny thing that becomes available.

When to transform

If an organisation is planning any kind of transformation, it must be clear why the change is necessary. It is important to

1: Introduction to High-velocity IT

think strategically, rather than following industry fashions and trends or making a change just because a competitor is doing the same thing.

Transformation is by its nature a major change, but it can (and arguably should) take place in an agile and incremental way. Transformation has costs and risks associated with it. Each organisation must be clear about:

- Whether funding is available;
- What the expected return on investment (ROI) is, and how it will be measured;
- If the level of risk is acceptable;
- If the required resources are available (or can be sourced); and
- If the transformation is aligned to the organisation's culture (or culture change is planned).

Good reasons to transform:

- It will deliver more value to customers.
- It will let you reach new markets.
- It will improve the employee experience in your organisation.
- It will save money, or allow you to achieve better quality for the same spend.

1: Introduction to High-velocity IT

> - It will improve the holistic customer experience, including a better consumer experience (CX) and user experience (UX).
>
> Not so good reasons to transform:
>
> - The new CIO said it was a good idea.
> - The CEO has a friend who runs a transformation consultancy organisation.
> - The salespeople at the conference were really persuasive…
>
> Extreme examples maybe, but it's estimated[2] that in 2019, $1.3 trillion was spent on digital transformation, and approximately $900 billion was wasted!

High-velocity IT objectives

There are five HVIT objectives:

- Valuable investments
- Fast development
- Resilient operations
- Value co-creation
- Assured conformance

Objective 1: Valuable investments

- Valuable investments result in a strategically innovative and effective application of IT.
- The organisation must identify where investments will make a contribution to business strategy, using utility to

---

[2] Source: Harvard Business Review, *https://hbr.org/2019/03/digital-transformation-is-not-about-technology*.

determine potential value and warranty to demonstrate that value can be delivered.
- Products need to be evaluated to assess their likely profitability, using research and development practices to avoid waste.
- The valuable investment objective would be addressed in the engage, plan and improve activities of the service value chain.

Objective 2: Fast development

- Fast development allows new products and services to be delivered frequently, reliably and at speed.
- Value is only realised when a product is delivered, so speed is important.
- Incremental development can help to ensure there is no trade-off between speed and quality – speed on its own has no value, it must be related to value co-creation when a product or service is used.
- In the service value chain, fast development activities would be found in the engage, design and transition, obtain/build, and improve activities.

Objective 3: Resilient operations

Resilient operations ensures digital products are available for use, allowing value to be realised. IT systems are complex, so failure cannot always be prevented. The service provider needs to focus on restoring service and delivering a level of warranty that protects the utility of the service. Resilient operations moves away from concepts like a single root

1: Introduction to High-velocity IT

cause of failure and focuses on protecting the value of investments.

The resilient operations objective would be addressed in the engage, deliver and support, and improve activities of the service value chain.

Objective 4: Co-created value

Value co-creation is based on effective interaction between the consumer and the service provider. This is linked to the ITIL 4 guiding principles 'Focus on Value' and 'Collaborate and Promote Visibility'. Users must be able to understand how digital products and services support their business activities in order to use them fully.

In the service value chain, co-created value is addressed in the engage, deliver and support, and improve activities.

Objective 5: Assured conformance

Products and services must comply with relevant legislation, regulations and corporate directives. These often relate to governance, risk and compliance.

HVIT is often seen as risky, but in fact approaches like DevOps are now used in highly monitored organisations such as banks. For conformance to be achieved, everyone in the organisation must understand what constraints are in place. The assured conformance objective is addressed by all service value chain activities as well as the governance component in the service value system.

1: Introduction to High-velocity IT

Think about IT initiatives you've seen in your career, or at the organisation where you currently work. Did they meet all, or some, of the HVIT objectives? Do you see any patterns between achievement of these objectives and the outcome of the IT initiative?

CHAPTER 2: THE DIGITAL PRODUCT LIFECYCLE AND THE ITIL OPERATING MODEL

The content in this chapter relates to:

- The four dimensions of service management;
- Volatility, uncertainty, complexity and ambiguity (VUCA);
- The digital product lifecycle;
- The ITIL service value system (SVS); and
- The service value chain.

The four dimensions of service management

Table 1 shows how the four dimensions of service management each relate to HVIT.

Table 1: HVIT and the Four Dimensions of Service Management

Organisations and people	HVIT is not just about technology. It has a significant impact on people too. In a High-velocity organisation, IT and business staff often work in the same space, known as co-location. However, there might still be some kind of central IT function for services like storage and email. There are no service level agreements (SLAs) between IT and the business because everyone is working as part of the same team. In some High-velocity organisations, there are 'digital

2: The digital product lifecycle and the ITIL operating model

	teams' and job titles like Chief Digital Officer.
Information and technology	HVIT places a greater demand on information and technology resources. Information is an essential resource, requiring IT teams to be aware of what data and information they have and how it can be used. The use of technology such as artificial intelligence (AI) and machine learning (ML) is ineffective without good information technology practices, for example the use of knowledge management to validate the data that is used by AI systems. Real-time information will become more important in an HVIT environment to support fast decision making.
Partners and suppliers	HVIT affects the supplier relationships an organisation enters into. High-velocity organisations will often use cloud services and infrastructure, and Software as a Service (SaaS) products. These can be highly affordable and will allow service providers to scale their products when necessary. The supplier relationship with these providers needs managing, but many of these services are offered in a 'one size fits all' way, so there is little customisation, and the relationship management can be fairly

2: The digital product lifecycle and the ITIL operating model

	low effort. The High-velocity organisation needs to be sure it understands its dependencies and has workarounds in place for risk scenarios (for example, a supplier ceasing trading).
Value streams and processes	Non-High-velocity organisations may have a single value stream or may not understand the concept of a value stream at all. High-velocity organisations typically create value streams for each product and service to allow them to be analysed and improved individually. This may be more resource intensive than creating a single value stream, but the effectiveness benefits should outweigh the additional costs. High-velocity organisations have operating models based on multiple value streams.

Looking at HVIT and the four dimensions of service management gives a holistic view of technology and its impact on the whole organisation. However, changing the way we think about every element of how we work can be daunting and result in mental paralysis. When I work with organisations that are going through a transformation or looking at embedding a continual improvement culture, I

2: The digital product lifecycle and the ITIL operating model

> normally encourage them to use their own resources and encourage their staff to come up with new ideas.
>
> From an HVIT perspective, though, I do sometimes suggest engaging with some outside organisations – either formally as consultants or informally by attending webinars, meet-ups, etc. There are many amazing smaller consultancy firms that have built deep expertise in areas like value stream mapping. Learning from their techniques can really accelerate your organisational learning curve. The use of a 'virtual consultancy practice' like the one I established at Scopism can provide access to mentoring and support services in a cost-effective, ad hoc way that aligns well with a High-velocity organisation.

The VUCA environment

The modern service management practitioner has to accept that their environment is now 'VUCA':

- **Volatile:** the nature, speed and dynamics of change.
- **Uncertain:** a lack of predictability, prospects of surprise.
- **Complex:** many forces, confounding issues, no cause/effect chain.
- **Ambiguous:** a haziness of reality, easy to misread, mixed meanings.

These elements create managerial challenges. Managers can respond to the challenges of a VUCA world by using more evolutionary approaches and being less reliant on long-term plans.

2: The digital product lifecycle and the ITIL operating model

Think about the country or industry that you work in. What has happened recently that has made your world more 'VUCA'? How have you, or your organisation, responded?

The digital product lifecycle

The service provider and the service consumer each have their own 'digital product lifecycle', which overlap during the period of their engagement.

Figure 1: Customer journey model[3]

During **exploration**, the consumer looks for possible solutions, and the provider explores opportunities and seeks customers. When a service provider and a service consumer discover each other, they **engage**, which may lead to a transaction. This transaction includes two activities of the customer journey: **offer** and **agree**.

Onboarding needs to take place before a service can be provided or consumed (**co-creation** of value); then value is **realised** if the consumer and provider's needs are met.

---

[3] *ITIL® 4: High-velocity IT*, figure 2.12. Copyright © AXELOS Limited 2020. Used under permission of AXELOS Limited. All rights reserved.

2: The digital product lifecycle and the ITIL operating model

This is a simplified version of the customer journey that is covered in much greater detail in the *ITIL® 4: Drive Stakeholder Value* publication. You can see more detail in the following table:

Table 2: Stages of the Digital Product Lifecycle[4]

Lifecycle stage	Service provider	Service consumer
Exploration	The service provider researches and develops the product and service offering.	The service consumer becomes aware of the existence of a product and assesses it as interesting and then desirable, after which an agreement is made.
Onboarding	An instance of the product is installed, and the user organisation is onboarded, sometimes with a transition from a replaced product.	
Co-creating value	The service provider delivers and supports the product and experiences	The service consumer uses the product and experiences increasing, stable,

---

[4] *ITIL® 4: High-velocity IT*, table 2.4. Copyright © AXELOS Limited 2020. Used under permission of AXELOS Limited. All rights reserved.

2: The digital product lifecycle and the ITIL operating model

	increasing, stable, or decreasing return on investment, leading to an investment decision to buy (use and improve the product), hold (use but do not improve it), or sell (use and reduce, replace, or retire it).	*or decreasing value, eventually leading to a decision to replace or retire the product.*
Offboarding	*The instance of the product is uninstalled and the user organisation is offboarded, sometimes with a transition to a replacement product.*	
Retired	*The service provider no longer offers or supports the product.*	*The service consumer no longer uses this product, but other consumers may use it.*

The service value system

The elements of the ITIL 4 service value system (SVS) are shown in the figure below:

2: The digital product lifecycle and the ITIL operating model

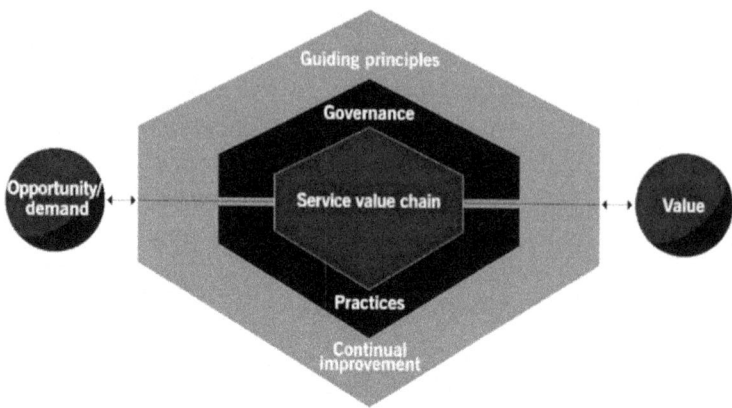

Figure 2: The ITIL service value system[5]

HVIT will have an impact on an organisation's governance and management. In digitally enabled organisations, you will often find that:

- IT is embedded in business or product teams, not structured as a separate unit;
- There is a unit or team responsible for digital technology and its use; and
- Practitioners use the governance and management framework to understand the constraints that apply to their work and the scope of their ability to make decisions within that framework.

---

[5] *ITIL® 4: High-velocity IT*, figure 2.9. Copyright © AXELOS Limited 2020. Used under permission of AXELOS Limited. All rights reserved.

2: The digital product lifecycle and the ITIL operating model

Where are the IT staff in your organisation chart? Are they a single business unit or department? Are IT skills embedded in business and product teams?

Banksbest has created a new digital team that operates outside the existing business divisions. What are the pros and cons of doing this?

An HVIT operating model is centralised around the use of digital technology in the co-creation of value. An operating model is *"a conceptual and/or visual representation of how an organisation co-creates value with its customers and other stakeholders, as well as how the organisation runs itself"*.

The HVIT operating model is characterised by:

- *"Dedicated value streams for each product and service*
- *Co-creational culture fostering high performance and continual improvement*
- *Permanent product/service teams rather than temporary teams*
- *Automated IT processes, including infrastructure as code."*

2: The digital product lifecycle and the ITIL operating model

"If you can't measure something, you can't understand it. If you can't understand it, you can't control it. If you can't control it, you can't improve it."[6]

The HVIT focus on value streams will allow organisations to visualise how they work, and how their products deliver value. I have seen myself how teams can make huge improvements by simply drawing out a process on a whiteboard or piece of paper.

Methodologies like OBASHI[7] can be used to visualise data flow in an organisation, again leading to understanding and improvement. As teams become more geographically dispersed, tools like Miro[8] allow collaboration to take place virtually.

An effective HVIT operating model should lead to high-performing teams that have the time and the motivation to visualise and improve what they do, and how they do it. This time is created for them by identifying and automating 'toil' and repeated tasks.

---

[6] Dr H. James Harrington.
[7] https://obashi.co.uk/.
[8] https://miro.com/.

2: The digital product lifecycle and the ITIL operating model

The service value chain

Service consumers may interact with multiple providers to get the service that they need (think about your mobile phone and the apps and streaming services you use with it).

Figure 3[9] shows how these multiple providers interact with an individual service provider's value chain. The service consumer has created an overall value chain that interacts with the service provider's value chain.

---

[9] *ITIL® 4: High-velocity IT*, figure 2.14. Copyright © AXELOS Limited 2020. Used under permission of AXELOS Limited. All rights reserved.

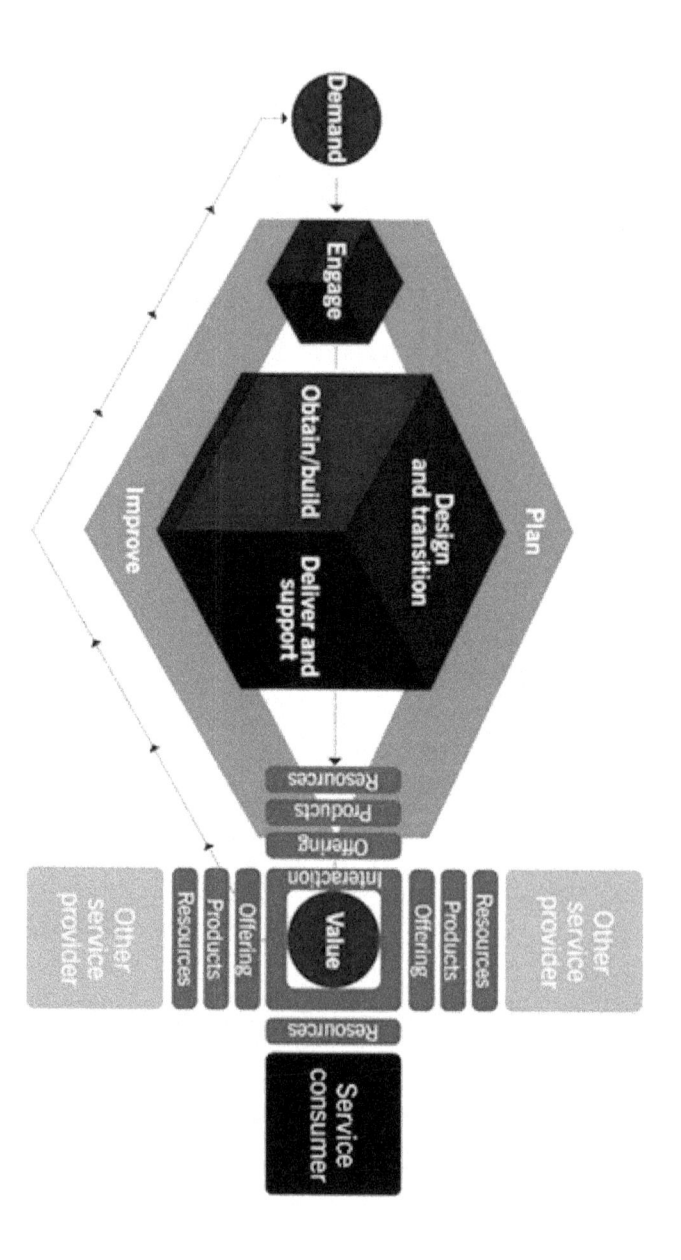

2: The digital product lifecycle and the ITIL operating model

Figure 3: The ITIL service value chain

2: The digital product lifecycle and the ITIL operating model

DevOps is often used to deliver High-velocity information technology. Figure 4 shows how the service value chain is applied in a DevOps environment. Note how the service value chain activities have been split into 'sub-activities' in order to map correctly to DevOps activities.

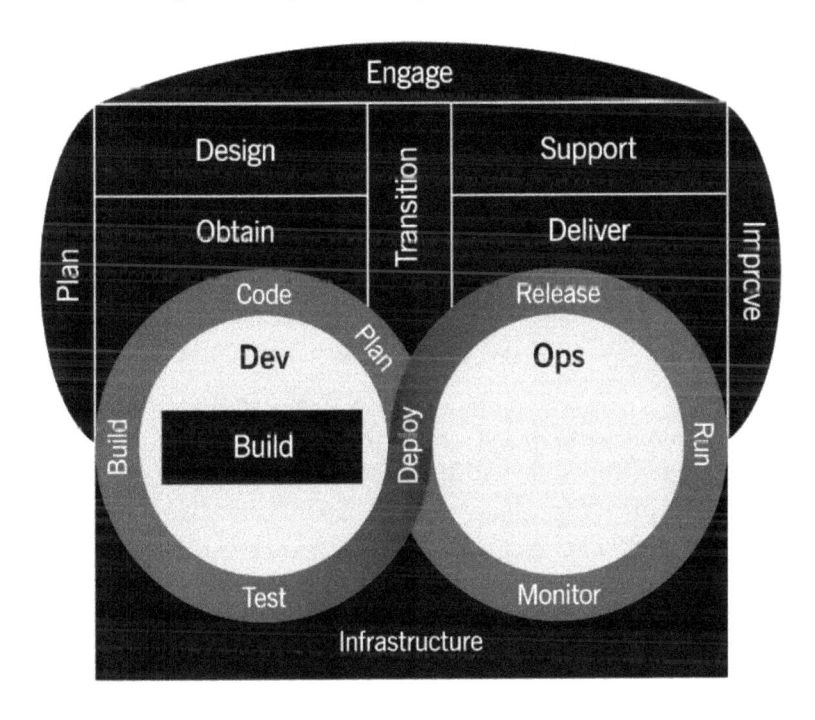

Figure 4: DevOps and the service value chain[10]

---

[10] *ITIL® 4: High-velocity IT*, figure 2.16. Copyright © AXELOS Limited 2020. Used under permission of AXELOS Limited. All rights reserved.

2: The digital product lifecycle and the ITIL operating model

DevOps describes a way of working that brings development (Dev) and operations (Ops) activities closer together. In many organisations, development and operations teams have a poor relationship. Development teams are accused of throwing solutions 'over the wall' and leaving operations to clean up the mess. Operations teams are accused of being obstructive, and slow to provide developers with the resources that they need to carry out their role. In my experience, the truth usually lies somewhere in the middle.

DevOps aims to build better relationships between Dev and Ops and as a result, deliver better software more quickly. DevOps has a large, highly engaged global community who share knowledge and continually create new ideas (for example, site reliability engineering (SRE)). There has also been some tension between DevOps and 'traditional' ITIL ways of working that reflects the Dev vs. Ops mentality. ITIL stereotypes such as needing a change advisory board and three weeks' notice to make a change have been used to suggest that ITIL is the antithesis of continuous delivery and deployment. Again, my experience suggests the truth is somewhere in the middle. Many organisations have a strong service management foundation with effective, repeatable processes. This gives them a stable environment to start experimenting with new ways of

2: The digital product lifecycle and the ITIL operating model

> working like DevOps and deliver better value to their customers.

> When I first started working with DevOps practitioners, I loved the idea of the hackathon, where people get together to work on a particular idea or piece of functionality. I applied this to ITSM to create the 'process hackathon'. If you've got a process or an area of IT in your organisation that is causing complaints and poor relationships, get everyone in a room (virtual room if necessary) and hack it! If change management is seen as slowing down development, get your developers on board and see what you can do together to build a better way of working. Hopefully you'll come out with some quick wins, and more importantly, some stronger relationships.

"*The service value chain activities link to the DevOps model…in the following ways:*

- *The design value chain activity runs in parallel with Dev, focusing more on the service than the software product.*
- *The obtain value chain activity is the interface with external Dev, integrating the developed software product with the other resources that the service comprises.*

2: The digital product lifecycle and the ITIL operating model

- *The build value chain activity corresponds to internal Dev.*
- *The transition value chain activity runs in parallel with, and corresponds to, the deployment from Dev to Ops.*
- *The deliver and support value chain activity corresponds to Ops and is often more comprehensive than Ops.*
- *The engage value chain activity runs in parallel with all of the underlying activities.*
- *The plan value chain activity corresponds to the planning part of Dev.*
- *The improve value chain activity corresponds to one of the tenets of DevOps: continual experimentation, learning, and improvement across all DevOps activities (often referred to as the 'Third Way' of DevOps)."*

Service consumer

In an HVIT environment, the provider and consumer interact in a very specific manner. Consumer demand creates requirements and engages a provider. The provider translates the requirements into a service, and value is co-created through the service use.

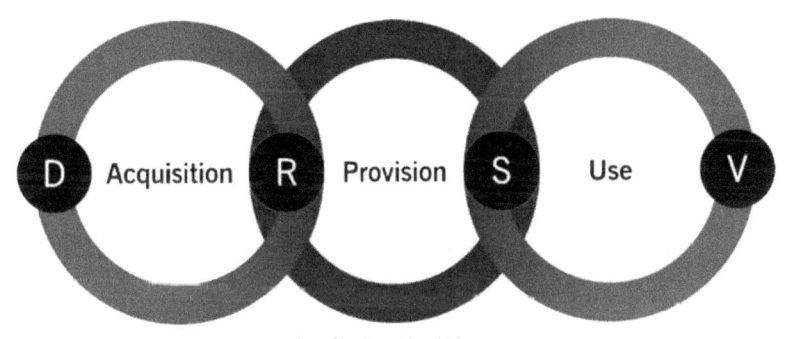

2: The digital product lifecycle and the ITIL operating model

D = Demand   R = Requirements   S = Service   V = Value

Figure 5: The service consumer's perspective[11]

The next figure shows the provider's value chain activities. Note that design and transition are in the top half, and delivery and support are in the bottom half. The same relationship exists between the consumer and provider through the activities of demand, requirements, product, service and value. Note the flow of the value stream through the value chain activities.

---

[11] *ITIL® 4: High-velocity IT*, figure 2.17. Copyright © AXELOS Limited 2020. Used under permission of AXELOS Limited. All rights reserved.

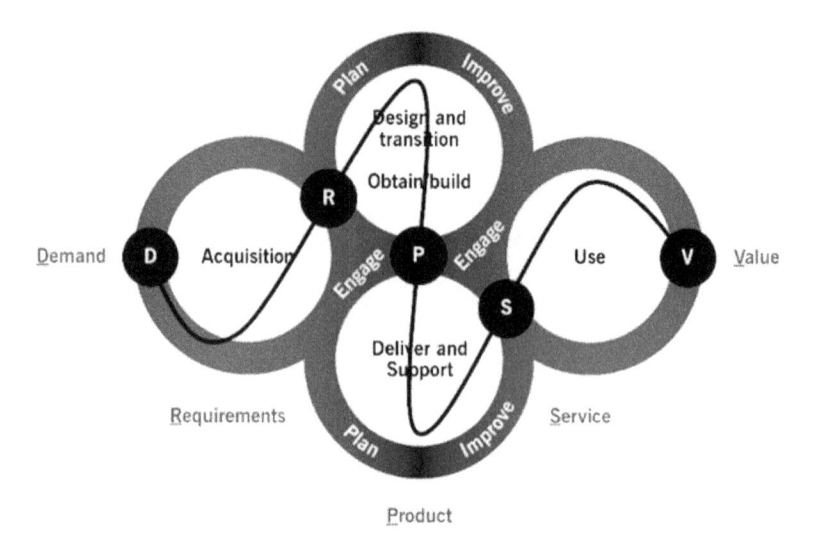

2: The digital product lifecycle and the ITIL operating model

Figure 6: Example value stream referring to service value chain activities[12]

Value streams

Value streams comprise a series of steps to create and deliver products and services to a consumer. Remember that a value chain describes the activities to manage products and services. Note the sets of activities in the figure 7.

---

[12] *ITIL® 4: High-velocity IT*, figure 2.19. Copyright © AXELOS Limited 2020. Used under permission of AXELOS Limited. All rights reserved.

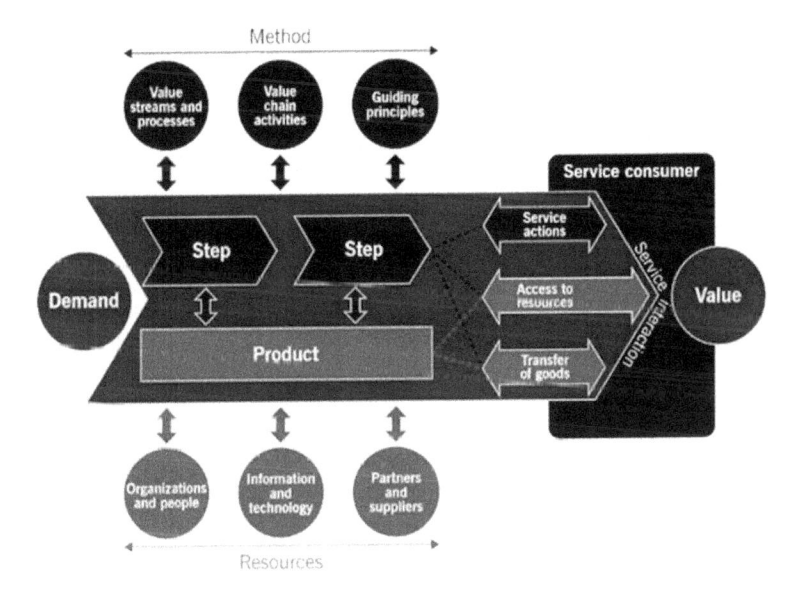

2: The digital product lifecycle and the ITIL operating model

Figure 7: The value stream in context[13]

What is not shown within the diagram above are three key elements:

- Governance
- Execution (managing and resourcing sub-elements)
- Improvement

These three concepts interact (in other words, governance applies to both execution and improvement; improvement applies to both governance and execution). In execution, operations is managed and has appropriate resources. Figure

---

[13] *ITIL® 4: High-velocity IT*, figure 2.20. Copyright © AXELOS Limited 2020. Used under permission of AXELOS Limited. All rights reserved.

2: The digital product lifecycle and the ITIL operating model

8[14] shows the value stream positioned with respect to governance, execution and improvement.

---

[14] *ITIL® 4: High-velocity IT*, figure 2.21. Copyright © AXELOS Limited 2020. Used under permission of AXELOS Limited. All rights reserved.

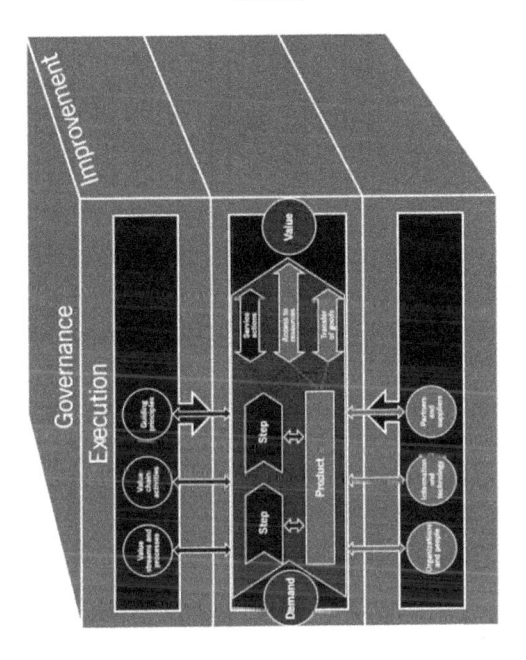

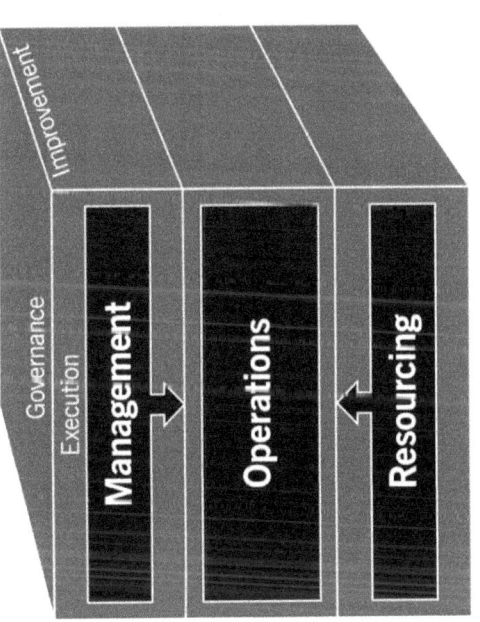

2: The digital product lifecycle and the ITIL operating model

Figure 8: Value stream positioned with respect to governance, execution, and improvement

2: The digital product lifecycle and the ITIL operating model

> Corporate governance defines why an organisation exists, which then defines how it is directed and controlled. Governance cascades down through the organisation, and decisions at every level should ultimately link back to the organisation's goals. If the purpose of the organisation isn't clear, it's very hard to improve how we work, because we don't know what we are trying to achieve. The decision to move towards a HVIT organisation can only be made within the context of the organisation's governance.
>
> I've worked with many organisations where governance isn't understood outside the boardroom. This makes it much harder for people at all levels to fulfil their roles and to make the right decisions.

CHAPTER 3: HVIT KEY BEHAVIOURS

This chapter will allow you to understand the five HVIT key behaviours:

- Accept ambiguity and uncertainty.
- Trust and be trusted.
- Continually raise the bar.
- Help to get customers' jobs done.
- Commit to continual learning.

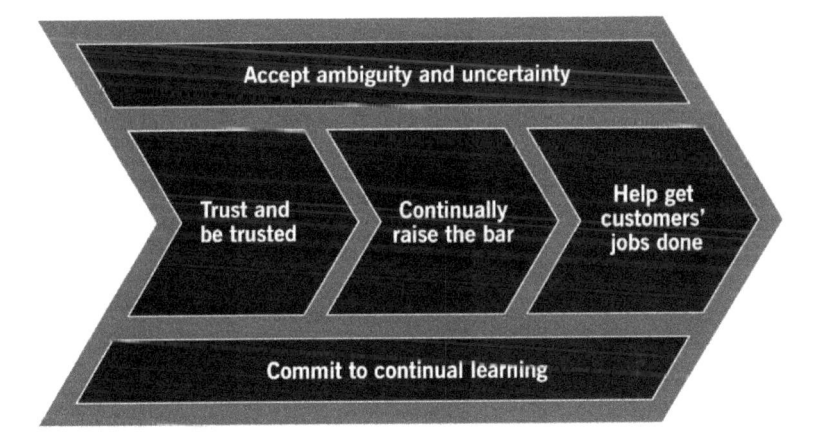

Figure 9: Key behavior patterns[15]

Five key behaviours are defined for HVIT. They support people working in digitally enabled organisations. Table 3

---

[15] *ITIL® 4: High-velocity IT*, figure 3.1. Copyright © AXELOS Limited 2020. Used under permission of AXELOS Limited. All rights reserved.

3: HVIT key behaviours

shows a mapping of the key behaviours to ITIL's guiding principles and other models and concepts.

Table 3: Models and Concepts and Related Key Behavior Patterns[16]

	Accept ambiguity and uncertainty	Trust and be trusted	Continually raise the bar	Help get customers' jobs done	Commit to continual learning
Purpose					
Ethics	✔	✔	✔	✔	✔
Design thinking				✔	
People					
Reconstructing for service agility			✔		
Safety culture		✔			
Stress prevention		✔			
Progress					
Working in complex environments	✔				
Lean culture		✔	✔		✔
ITIL continual improvement model	✔		✔		✔

---

[16] *ITIL® 4: High-velocity IT*, table 3.1. Copyright © AXELOS Limited 2020. Used under permission of AXELOS Limited. All rights reserved.

3: HVIT key behaviours

ITIL guiding principles					
Focus on value				✔	
Start where you are	✔				
Progress iteratively with feedback	✔				✔
Collaborate and promote visibility		✔			
Think and work holistically	✔				
Keep it simple and practical			✔		
Optimize and automate			✔		

Behaviour 1: Accept ambiguity and uncertainty

Technology changes, customer requirements change, the environment changes, people change. To deal with uncertainty, organisations need to adopt an experiment-based approach. People should be allowed to fail without being punished, treating failure as a learning experience.

Supporting guiding principles: progress iteratively with feedback, start where you are, think and work holistically.

3: HVIT key behaviours

Behaviour 2: Trust and be trusted

People are at the heart of technical teams. To work effectively, organisations need to create a culture that trusts people to make decisions and supports knowledge sharing. In this type of organisation, people are comfortable sharing honest feedback, and treat their colleagues as human beings.

Supporting guiding principle: collaborate and promote visibility.

Behaviour 3: Continually raise the bar

Higher performance is about a focus on continually raising the bar. It is delivered by improving both velocity and quality. Organisations need to encourage all their staff to identify improvements, no matter how small, and contribute to getting them done.

Supporting guiding principles: keep it simple and practical, optimize and automate.

Behaviour 4: Help to get customers' jobs done

Helping customers to get jobs done is about creating products and services that help customers solve problems and carry out their role or live their life.

Supporting guiding principle: focus on value.

Behaviour 5: Commit to continual learning

A commitment to continual learning is a key part of a digital organisation. This can include knowledge discovery, knowledge sharing, and seeking out new ways to deliver products and services. This key behaviour underpins all the other key behaviours.

3: HVIT key behaviours

Supporting guiding principle: progress iteratively with feedback.

Here's a reminder of the key HVIT behaviours:

- Accept ambiguity and uncertainty.
- Trust and be trusted.
- Continually raise the bar.
- Help to get customers' jobs done.
- Commit to continual learning.

Do you see any evidence of these in the Banksbest case study? Which of the key behaviours do you think is the most important for Banksbest and its current strategy?

CHAPTER 4: PRINCIPLES, MODELS AND CONCEPTS

There are numerous principles, models and concepts that might be applied in High-velocity organisations. These principles, models and concepts are applied to help support the HVIT behaviours we outlined in the previous chapter. The principles, models and concepts we'll review in this chapter are:

- Ethics
- Safety culture
- Lean culture
- Toyota Kata
- Lean/Agile/resilient/continuous
- Service-dominant logic
- Design thinking
- Complexity thinking

> The ITIL 4 Specialist High-velocity IT syllabus covers a lot of topics but without going into them in great detail. There are some ideas here that will be exciting and relevant to your career. I would recommend making a note of any areas where you want to do further study once you've passed your exam.

4: Principles, models and concepts

Ethics

"Ethics is a system of principles that defines what is good for individuals and society."

The political, environmental, social and economic impact of IT is increasing. Digital organisations should consider it a moral obligation to consider the impact of their products and services, beyond their own economic interests. Software engineering and social engineering are becoming strongly linked as software becomes more embedded in our daily lives. Social engineering can have both positive and negative connotations. It is broadly defined as describing how social change and behaviour can be influenced or managed centrally (for example, by a government), but it is also used in the IT security context to describe how bad actors can influence people into revealing confidential or personal information.

Organisations that are concerned about behaving ethically need to consider:

- How do their actions affect others?
- Can they establish and embed some generic ethical principles? And how do they deal with situations where the principles don't apply?
- Can they create a space to discuss dilemmas?
- Do they accept responsibility for choosing the 'least bad' course of action?

Consider how ethics contributes to the key HVIT behaviours:

- **Trust and be trusted**

4: Principles, models and concepts

Behaving ethically builds trust within an organisation. People feel more comfortable sharing their thoughts and feelings.

- **Accept ambiguity and uncertainty**
  The impact of a product or service might not be fully understood until it is delivered; ethical principles will help an organisation deal with unintended consequences.

> Can you think of any tech industry stories you've seen in the news recently that raise ethical questions? Do some research if none come to mind immediately. What can tech companies do to ensure they behave more ethically?
>
> Many tech stories are reported by news outlets in a way that blames technology, often mentioning 'the algorithm'. What would be a more accurate way to report these stories?

Safety culture

"Safety culture is a climate in which people are comfortable being (and expressing) themselves."

Increasing pressure to deliver products and services quickly can lead to burnout and stress. Organisations need to:

4: Principles, models and concepts

- Encourage behaviour that is good for all stakeholders, including employees; and
- Foster shared beliefs, perceptions and values.

In a safety culture, people will feel comfortable expressing themselves, feel trusted and valued, and feel safe to point out risks and issues. Management needs to commit to the concept of a safety culture and 'walk the walk' when it comes to demonstrating good behaviours.

There are links between a safety culture and complex systems. In complex systems:

- They always have multiple flaws and latent issues; continual changes mean flaws continually change;
- Most flaws are small, because of system resilience or human intervention;
- Significant issues happen due to unpredictable combinations of flaws, not due to a single root cause;
- Dealing with issues requires knowledge, skills and good working conditions:
  - Safe working conditions are critical when things get stressful.
  - Culture needs to embrace 'not blaming people' and 'failure is an improvement opportunity'.
- People need confidence to share opinions and experiment.

Behaviour patterns associated with safety culture include the following:

- Don't just talk about why safety is important, do something about it.

4: Principles, models and concepts

- Exhibit vulnerability: say when you have doubts and ask for help.
- Foster feedback and act on it.
- Be kind and compassionate: build human relationships.
- Be realistic about failure: acknowledge that it will happen, and that the system is to blame, not people.

Consider how a safety culture contributes to the key HVIT behaviours.

- **Commit to continual learning:** A safety culture allows staff to ask uncomfortable questions that can unlock additional value.
- **Help to get customers' jobs done:** People feel safe talking to customers, sharing problems and working together to co-create value.

> Some of the cultural issues in the Banksbest case study would inhibit feelings of safety. What are they? What could Lucy Jones do to try to overcome them and improve the likelihood of her project succeeding?

Lean culture

"A Lean culture is characterized as a work environment where trust, respect, curiosity, inquiry, playfulness and intensity all co-exist to support learning and discovery."

4: Principles, models and concepts

Lean culture is different than Lean thinking:

"Lean thinking is a business methodology that aims to provide a new way to think about how to organize human activities to deliver more benefits to society and value to individuals while eliminating waste. Lean thinking, based on the Toyota Production System, is a way of thinking about an activity and seeing the waste inadvertently generated by the way the process is organized."[17]

Lean culture supports HVIT by creating an environment that is effective, resilient and adaptable. Lean culture allows Lean tools to be applied in context. Leaders set norms and expectations in a Lean culture, which inspires engagement from staff. Review table 4 for the elements of a Lean culture.

Table 4: Elements of Lean Culture[18]

Trust	*The assured reliance on the character, ability, strength, or truth of someone or something, including a team, a work process, and, most importantly, process.*
Respect	*The act of giving particular attention, consideration, special regard, and esteem to another.*
Curiosity	*A relentless desire to know how and why things work, what makes things work better, and what 'better' looks like after things have been made better.*

---

[17] *https://en.wikipedia.org/wiki/Lean_thinking.*
[18] *ITIL® 4: High-velocity IT*, table 3.2. Copyright © AXELOS Limited 2020. Used under permission of AXELOS Limited. All rights reserved.

4: Principles, models and concepts

Enquiry	*A systematic search for the facts about the nature of things: their origins, their causes, their interdependencies, their lifecycles, and their nature.*
Playfulness	*A fresh, fun way of viewing ideas and their relationship to other ideas while simultaneously maintaining serious focus.*
Intensity	*A deep focus on the topic at hand, and the persistence not to become distracted or lose the path.*

Adopting a Lean culture requires organisational leaders to make changes to their behaviour too. First, they need to clearly understand the goal for the organisation, so that they can shape the culture and provide focus areas for their teams and direct reports. Lean leaders need to create a safe environment for frontline staff, so that everyone in the organisation has time to try new things and learn from any mistakes. This is very different to traditional 'command and control' leadership.

Lean leaders need to act as coaches, asking questions and offering help rather than telling people what to do. They should reinforce good behaviours.

There are several behaviours that will develop a Lean culture. They include:

- Trusting people and the system but being vigilant and providing feedback ('trust but verify');
- Treating others as you would like to be treated;

4: Principles, models and concepts

- Understanding how things work and looking for improvements;
- Challenging hypotheses with gathered facts;
- Developing insights with creativity and exploration; and
- Focusing on the topic.

Consider how Lean culture contributes to the key HVIT behaviours.

- **Continually raise the bar:** The inquiry and intensity elements of Lean culture help people to focus on the goal of higher performance.
- **Commit to continual learning:** The curiosity element of Lean culture will support this HVIT behaviour.

A Lean culture is characterised among other things by curiosity, inquiry, playfulness and intensity. Some of this terminology doesn't fit with the organisations that many of us are accustomed to working with. For some cultures (British included), the idea of 'play' at work can be off-putting and alarming. It's important for organisations to analyse their current environment, people and culture and then think about what will work for them.

One pattern I have seen is organisations that adopt the 'theatre' of a new culture without actually changing anything. Their offices are filled with toys, slides, comfy chairs...but no one feels comfortable using them. I

4: Principles, models and concepts

> worked with one organisation that had a pool table hidden inside the boardroom table – as long as I worked there, I never saw anyone use it. Remember that culture change is about changing what is innate to us; although the trappings can be useful, we mustn't get carried away with sticky notes and trying to force people to have fun.

Toyota Kata

"Toyota Kata is a mental model and behaviour pattern for scientific thinking and routines for practice and coaching."

Toyota Kata supports organisational improvement through:

- Scientific thinking and disciplined execution;
- A focus on 'unlearning' old habits (unlearning means to discard something learned, especially a bad habit or false or outdated information from one's memory);
- Practice and coaching; and
- Creating confidence and competence to improve.

Toyota Kata is a four-step improvement process, based on five questions (see figure 10):

1. What are we trying to achieve?
2. Where are we now?
3. What obstacle is now in our way?
4. What's our next step, and what do we expect?
5. When can we see what we've learned from taking that step?

4: Principles, models and concepts

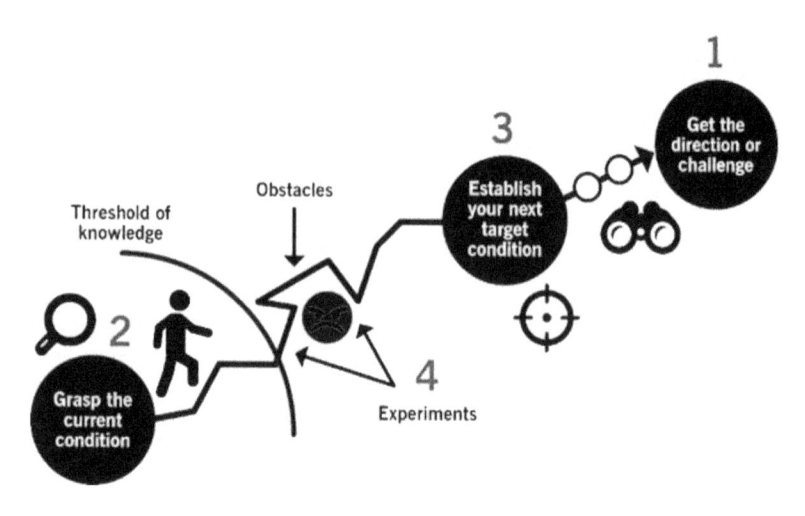

Figure 10: Toyota Kata[19]

Lean/Agile/resilient/continuous

"Lean, agile, resilient and continuous are dominant characteristics of common High-velocity IT approaches."

Lean

Lean helps to improve throughput and reduce waste by breaking down large pieces of work into smaller pieces; Kanban boards are useful when managing work in this way as they help to visualise work in progress.

Agile

Agile adds close and iterative collaboration in HVIT, based on ongoing conversations between users and developers.

---

[19] *ITIL® 4: High-velocity IT*, figure 3.12. Copyright © AXELOS Limited 2020. Used under permission of AXELOS Limited. All rights reserved.

4: Principles, models and concepts

Resilience

Resilience maintains workable availability and performance through practices such as DevSecOps and site reliability engineering (SRE).

> Our ways of working in IT are always evolving. DevOps is fairly unique in the IT world as it has no core text associated with it – no one owns it, and new DevOps ideas continually spring from its active community.
>
> I remember going to a DevOps meet-up some years ago and hearing about 'BizDevOps', an approach that embraces Dev and Ops teams but also adds in the business users. One would hope they were there already, but BizDevOps made it explicit.
>
> DevSecOps focuses on including security in every element of the development process; again, one would hope it was already there, but it's good to make it explicit. DevSecOps is growing, and you'll find plenty of information and resources online if this is a relevant area to you.

Continuous

'Continuous' ensures fast and reliable deployment and uses techniques including continuous integration (CI) and continuous delivery (CD).

4: Principles, models and concepts

Consider how Lean/Agile/resilient/continuous contribute to the key HVIT behaviours.

- **Commit to continual learning:**
  CI/CD and Agile allow more frequent increments and improvements to products and services.
- **Accept ambiguity and uncertainty:**
  Resilient services are more able to cope with changing environments.

CD describes an approach to software engineering where teams produce software in short cycles. This means that software can be released at any time and will work as expected. It supports software build, test and release at speed. It can also help to reduce the cost, time and risk of delivering changes by allowing production applications to be updated more frequently.

CI is a strategy that optimises for team productivity. There are frequent code commits (at least once a day) that create smaller batches of work. Gated commits are used to reject anything that takes the code away from a deployable state. CI creates fast feedback and makes failure visible.

Service-dominant logic

"Service-dominant logic is a mental model of an (economic) exchange in which organisations co-create value by applying their competencies and other resources for the benefit of each other."

Service-dominant logic is different to goods-dominant logic. In a goods-based transaction, the ownership of goods is transferred to the customer from the provider (the provider

4: Principles, models and concepts

delivers value). In a service transaction, value creation is collaborative, and value is co-created.

"Service science defines service as the application of resources (including competencies, skills, and knowledge) to make changes that have value for another. In any service there are at least two interacting entities, called service systems. Examples of service systems are service providers and service consumers, but there are usually other stakeholders as well, such as regulatory bodies. A core concept in service science is service-dominant logic."

Consider how service-dominant logic contributes to the key HVIT behaviours.

- **Help to get customers' jobs done:** Focus on service transactions and value co-creation helps to ensure service provider staff are aligned with customer requirements and act appropriately.
- **Trust and be trusted:** Seeing service provision as a long-term relationship based on value co-creation helps to build trust between consumer and service provider.

Design thinking

"Design thinking refers to the set of cognitive and practical processes by which design concepts are developed."

Design thinking includes five stages:
- **Empathise**: researching user needs.
- **Define**: stating user needs and problems.
- **Ideate**: challenging assumptions and creating ideas.
- **Prototype**: initial creation of solutions.
- **Test**: testing of the suggested solutions.

4: Principles, models and concepts

Design thinking helps practitioners to:

- Create better digital products;
- Create better customer experiences;
- Help get customers' jobs done; and
- Design user experiences, rather than goods.

Consider how design thinking contributes to the key HVIT behaviours.

- **Commit to continual learning:** Design thinking helps people to focus on the experience and the problems that a product or service is solving, supporting better design and better products and services.
- **Continually raise the bar:** A focus on customer experiences will support value co-creation, leading to a better relationship with consumers and the ability to identify and create more value.

Complexity thinking

Complex systems are unpredictable and can be a challenge to the people working with them. An experimental approach is required for both development and support, including:

- Many independent experiments in parallel;
- Dealing with the negative side-effects of experiments that fail; and
- Continuing and broadening experiments that succeed.

Cynefin is a sense-making framework to help organisations deal with complexity. It includes five domains that characterise the relationship between cause and effect.

The five domains are defined below:

4: Principles, models and concepts

- *"Obvious[20] – clear causality, where predetermined best practice should be applied*
- *Complicated – unclear but knowable causality that can be determined by analysis or expertise, followed by good practice*
- *Complex – unclear and unknowable causality requiring safe-to-fail experimentation (emergent practice)*
- *Chaotic – a more extreme form of complexity that demands immediate action to transition the situation to complex (novel practice)*
- *Disorder – the state of not knowing in which of the other domains you are, with a bias to assume that the domain corresponds to the context in which you are most experienced."*

---

[20] The Cynefin framework was updated in 2020, with changes including the renaming of 'Obvious' to 'Clear'. See www.cognitive-edge.com/ for more detail.

4: Principles, models and concepts

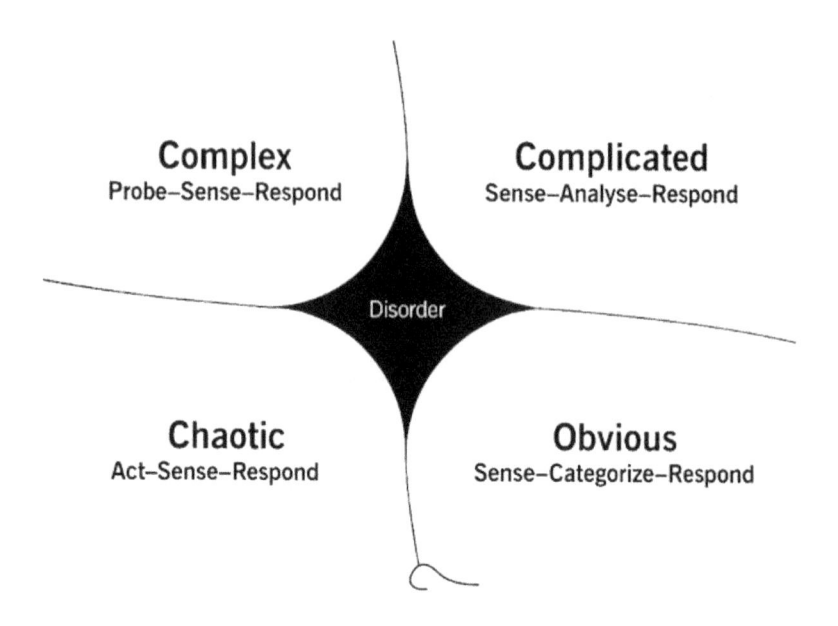

```
      Complex              Complicated
  Probe–Sense–Respond    Sense–Analyse–Respond

                Disorder

      Chaotic                Obvious
   Act–Sense–Respond   Sense–Categorize–Respond
```

Figure 11: The Cynefin framework[21]

Applying complexity thinking can help people avoid assumptions and think beyond rigid processes and plans. Unpredictability is not always negative and can lead to innovation. To troubleshoot a complex failure, organisations will:

- Identify hypotheses for what might be happening;
- In parallel, test each plausible hypothesis, using small, safe-to-fail experiments;
- Observe the impact of the experiments; and
- Try to amplify any positive outcomes, and dampen any negative effects.

---

[21] *ITIL® 4: High-velocity IT*, figure 3.7. Copyright © AXELOS Limited 2020. Used under permission of AXELOS Limited. All rights reserved.

4: Principles, models and concepts

Behaviour patterns that support complexity thinking include:

- Assessing causality, and being aware of natural bias;
- Acting according to the context (using guidance including frameworks such as Cynefin);
- Being wary of 'recipes' based on cases and so-called best practice; and
- Avoiding the desire to try to engineer human systems – evolve them, and move to the next 'adjacent possible'.

Complexity thinking can be challenging for people who are accustomed to following processes and procedures. It is associated with anti-fragile systems, which increase in capability, resilience and robustness as a response to stress or failure.

Consider how complexity thinking contributes to these key HVIT behaviours.

- **Continually raise the bar:** Complexity thinking supports experimentation and learning.
- **Trust and be trusted:** Complexity thinking encourages staff to think 'beyond the process' and find new ways to do things, allowing them to fail safely.

CHAPTER 5: ENSURING VALUABLE INVESTMENTS

This chapter addresses:

- How the service provider ensures the achievement of valuable investments; and
- How the service provider uses ITIL practices to achieve valuable investments.

Techniques for ensuring valuable investments

A service provider can ensure the achievement of valuable investments using a variety of techniques, including:

- Prioritisation
- Minimum viable products or services
- Product or service ownership
- A/B testing

To ensure investments in services deliver value, the service provider should confirm that the service contributes to the achievement of the service strategy. Contribution means that the potential value, costs, return on investment (ROI) and utility requirements are understood. Warranty is also defined but doesn't add to the value proposition of the product or service. Warranty is the 'guarantee' that the product or service is not adversely affected by outages or other affecting factors.

Table 5 shows the definitions of utility and warranty.

5: Ensuring valuable investments

Table 5: Utility and Warranty Definitions

Utility	*"Functionality offered by a product or a service to meet a particular need. Simply, it is 'what the product/service does' and determines if it is 'fit for purpose.'"*
Warranty	*"Assurance that the agreed product or service will meet agreed requirements. Simply, it is 'how the product/service performs' and determines if it is 'fit for use'."*

When determining valuable investments, market research is critical. Consider the impact and uptake of the digital product or service. The quality and timing of the release of the new product or service is also critical – the goal is to gain market share, build competitive advantage and increase market share.

Service providers need to evaluate investments to ensure they are fulfilling their expected outcomes, but also to capitalise on additional options that may exist. Commercial and non-profit organisations will look at valuable investments differently. Review table 6 to see how different types of organisation will measure valuable investments.

5: Ensuring valuable investments

Table 6: Measuring Valuable Investments

Commercial	Non-profit
Higher prices	Achievement of organisation-specific objectives
Reduced capital and operational costs	Revenues to cover costs of operation
Increased sales	Increased impact/achievement of outcomes
Reduced risk	Reduced risk
Increased revenue	Better return on investment

A valuable investment can only be determined when the return is realised, through the co-creation of value between the service provider, consumer and other stakeholders. As IT is the key driver in the digital organisation, it is important to consistently evaluate the potential of IT capabilities to ensure a strategic advantage.

The speed at which the valuable investment can be designed, developed and delivered is crucial in the digital organisation. There are a variety of techniques that help organisations to achieve valuable investments.

5: Ensuring valuable investments

Prioritisation

Prioritisation is used by organisations when demand exceeds supply. For example, the demand for a specific product or service exceeds the organisation's capacity to deliver it. There are several techniques to manage prioritisation, including:

Cost of delay
- The financial and non-financial (e.g. reputation, morale, etc.) areas that would be affected if the product or service activity was delayed. This technique focuses on the business criticality of the product or service.

Buy/hold/sell
- Apply the investment strategies of buy/hold/sell to the product or service to decide priority. The costs of developing, maintaining or retiring a product/service are described and now a knowledge-based decision can be made.
    - **Buy** – invest in improvement or continued offering of a product/service.
    - **Hold** – spend minimally to maintain the product/service (costs must be affordable).
    - **Sell** – invest in retiring, reducing, replacing the product/service.
- Other techniques include stacked ranking, Kano, net present value (NPV), ROI, fit/feasibility/attractiveness.

5: Ensuring valuable investments

> For the HVIT exam, you will only need to recognise the names of the techniques mentioned in the final bullet point above. If this is an area of interest for you, why not do additional research after your exam?

> Few IT or service management professionals work in an environment where there is ample time and unlimited resource to complete all tasks. In my experience, the ability to prioritise effectively is an essential skill. In organisations that lack formal prioritisation mechanisms, informal ways of working develop. These can be very frustrating for the team members carrying out the work, because prioritisation is based on who shouts loudest, or what work looks more interesting. If someone feels that the prioritisation is wrong, it's hard to appeal against a process that doesn't exist. You might, for example, have come across "Highest Paid Person's Opinion" or HiPPO prioritisation. This isn't an approach I'd recommend!

In the service value chain (SVC), the plan and improve activities have the strongest relationship with prioritisation.

5: Ensuring valuable investments

Which ITIL practices influence or use prioritisation? Review table 7, paying close attention to the high-impact practices, (**H** = high impact, **M** = medium impact and **L** = low impact).

Table 7: Practices for which Prioritisation is Relevant[22]

ITIL management practice	Activities/resources associated with prioritization	Impact
Portfolio management	*Continually prioritizing service offerings based on value, incorporating the cost of delay.*	H
Problem management	*Calculating the financial cost of open problems and errors in order to prioritize and direct problem management efforts.* *Comparing the costs of workarounds with those of longer-term solutions.*	H
Project management	*Calculating the financial impact of performing or delaying project work.*	H
Software development and management	*Calculating the financial impact of delaying work on new software features or larger software-based service components. Deciding whether to*	H

---

[22] *ITIL® 4: High-velocity IT*, table 4.1. Copyright © AXELOS Limited 2020. Used under permission of AXELOS Limited. All rights reserved.

5: Ensuring valuable investments

	obtain or build software components.	
Change enablement	*Calculating the cost and benefit of prioritizing and scheduling changes to services or service components.*	M
Incident management	*Calculating the cost of incidents and major incidents in order to prioritize work that has the highest economic impact.*	M
Release management	*Calculating the cost and benefit of prioritizing and scheduling releases of new or changed services.*	M
Service financial management	*Calculating time value profile data to provide information for prioritizing service offerings.*	M
Service request management	*Calculating and comparing the financial impact of fulfilling or delaying the fulfilment of requests in order to prioritize work with the highest benefit.*	L

Minimum viable products and services

A minimum viable product or service is *"one that has just enough features to enable its early assessment and the collection of feedback for future development"*.

5: Ensuring valuable investments

This is an expedient approach when market conditions are volatile or unpredictable – deliver a product or service with minimum features (it gets the job done) so the investment in that product or service is fiscally prudent. If, or when, the environment and requirements become more defined, then either continue or stop the investment.

The product should be good enough to generate feedback in order to make an informed decision. ITIL 4 defines these characteristics for a minimum viable product or service:

- *"Has enough value that people are willing to use or buy it*
- *Demonstrates enough potential benefits to retain early adopters*
- *Provides a feedback loop to guide future development."*

Within the service value chain, the activity of design and transition relates most strongly to this technique, and the minimum viable approach influences the design and transition activity at a high level.

There are several ITIL practices that also influence the minimum viable product and service technique for valuable investments. Review table 8, paying close attention to the high-impact practices.

5: Ensuring valuable investments

Table 8: Practices for Which a Minimal Viable Approach is Relevant[23]

ITIL management practice	Activities/resources associated with a minimum viable approach	Impact
Architecture management	Using a minimum viable approach to describe the service, technical, information, or environmental architecture that will create the necessary constraints, boundaries, or enablers for other types of service or product work.	H
Business analysis	Using a minimum viable approach as a tool to extract core business value from a product or service.	H
Capacity and performance management	Using capacity and performance management as a basis for calculating the minimum resources (number of servers, number of service desk agents, etc.) required for a minimum viable product or service.	H

---

[23] *ITIL® 4: High-velocity IT*, table 4.2. Copyright © AXELOS Limited 2020. Used under permission of AXELOS Limited. All rights reserved.

5: Ensuring valuable investments

Monitoring and event management	Using monitoring and event management as the basis for designing and configuring tools for monitoring and telemetry, which are used to operate and learn from the minimum viable product or service.	H
Portfolio management	Using the concept of a minimal viable product as a dynamic decision-making tool to support good investments in the portfolio of features within a product or service.	H
Project management	Articulating the minimum output needed to satisfy the business case.	H
Service design	Using a minimum viable approach to design the necessary customer experience and user experience elements of a product or service.	H
Service validation and testing	Developing test cases to check that all service components support the minimum viable product or service.	H
Software development	Using a minimum viable approach as a decision-making	H

5: Ensuring valuable investments

and management	*tool to prioritize work on software features.*	
Infrastructure and platform management	*Using a minimum viable approach as a decision-making tool to design, implement, and prioritize ongoing work on infrastructure components.*	*M*
Service catalogue management	*Using a minimum viable approach as a basis to describe all products, services, and service offerings, and ensuring this information is available to relevant audiences.*	*M*
Service continuity management	*Designing and building continuity plans to support a minimum viable product or service.*	*M*
Supplier management	*Using a minimum viable approach to articulate the outputs required when partners and suppliers provide products and services.*	*M*

Product or service ownership

Product or service ownership is critical to the High-velocity organisation. Ownership ensures the product or service is developed to maximise value, with defined priorities, in liaison with other stakeholders including customers. Without ownership, the product or service can drift away from the

5: Ensuring valuable investments

original plan or desired outcome. The HVIT environment is product or service-oriented, and this role depends on the following characteristics:

- **Skills and experience**: including a range of management skills and analytical skills, understanding of the market, as well as an understanding of Agile work methods.
- **Authority**: including having the authority to prioritise and communicate activities to support the lifecycle of the valuable investment. Most importantly, the organisation must trust the product or service owner to use their authority prudently.
- **Legitimacy**: the owner has to develop and demonstrate they have the necessary skills to capably prioritise projects.
- **Time**: this includes having the necessary time to fulfil all aspects of the role – including developing the user stories, managing the backlog, communicating with customers and stakeholders, leading the team and evaluating benefit realisation.

> Do product owner or service owner roles exist in your organisation? If they do, what benefits do you associate

5: Ensuring valuable investments

> with them? (If they don't exist, does that create any negative impact?)
>
> At Banksbest, Lucy Jones has been allocated the product owner role for the My Way project. Based on the information in the case study, what challenges does she face? What skills will she need to be successful in the role?

Every activity in the service value chain has a very strong relationship with the technique of product or service ownership. Table 9 provides information about the practices where product or service ownership is most relevant. Pay close attention to the high-impact practices.

Table 9: Practices for Which Product or Service Ownership Is Relevant[24]

ITIL management practice	Activities/resources associated with product or service ownership	Impact
Infrastructure and platform management	*Involvement of product and service owners in articulating, refining, and prioritizing the infrastructure and platform development backlog(s), and in deciding whether to acquire commercially available infrastructure components and services.*	H

---

[24] *ITIL® 4: High-velocity IT*, table 4.3. Copyright © AXELOS Limited 2020. Used under permission of AXELOS Limited. All rights reserved.

5: Ensuring valuable investments

Portfolio management	Involvement of (software) product owners and product or service managers in evaluating and prioritizing the product or service investment proposals.	H
Relationship management	Structuring interactions with stakeholders. Involvement in establishing customers' priorities for new or changed products and services. Coordinating customers' requirements and feedback. Involvement in addressing complaints and mediating conflicting requirements.	H
Service catalogue management	Involvement of product or service owners and managers in publishing information on all products, services, and service offerings.	H
Software development and management	Involvement of product and service owners in articulating, refining, and prioritizing the software development backlog, and in deciding whether to acquire or upgrade commercially available software.	H

5: Ensuring valuable investments

Project management	*Involvement of product and service owners and managers in delivering project work and managing risks.*	M
Risk management	*Involvement of product and service owners in articulating and mitigating enterprise risks.*	M
Supplier management	*Involvement of product and service owners and managers in articulating needs, structuring interactions, and negotiating with partners and suppliers.*	M

A/B testing

A/B testing is a *"time-limited experiment in which one group of users, the control group, is provided with an old version of a product or service. At the same time, another group of users, the treatment group, is provided with a new version of the product or service that includes the new feature."*

Assuming both groups are broadly the same, data can be gathered that allows a value-based decision, providing a prioritisation of work and important feedback.

A/B testing strongly contributes to the portfolio management practice by providing the necessary data to make an informed decision around investment.

Within the service value chain, the activities of improve and obtain/build have the strongest relationship to A/B testing.

5: Ensuring valuable investments

> I find now that many organisations (including my own) are making a concerted effort to base their decisions on data and evidence, rather than the gut feel or instinct of their staff. This is wise, and digital services allow us to collect huge amounts of data to support our decisions. We can track what links are clicked, where the mouse moves, even down to how different colours influence what people do with our products and services. It's important, though, to try to be as scientific as possible. It's easy to inadvertently look for data that reinforces what you believe, or to ask the wrong questions. Some study of the principles of data science or statistics can really change how you approach these activities.

Review table 10 for the practices that A/B testing is most relevant. Pay close attention to the high-impact practices.

5: Ensuring valuable investments

Table 10: Practices for Which A/B Testing Is Relevant[25]

ITIL management practice	Activities/resources associated with A/B testing	Impact
Portfolio management	Deciding and prioritizing which services, products, and features to invest in using A/B testing data.	H
Risk management	Using A/B testing methods to determine the effectiveness of risk mitigation options before making further investments.	H
Service design	Using A/B testing methods to determine the effectiveness of customer experience and user experience prototypes before making further investments and design decisions.	H
Architecture management	Designing and refining technical, information, product, and service architecture using A/B testing methods.	M

---

[25] *ITIL® 4: High-velocity IT*, table 4.4. Copyright © AXELOS Limited 2020. Used under permission of AXELOS Limited. All rights reserved.

5: Ensuring valuable investments

Continual improvement	Using A/B testing methods to determine the effectiveness of various improvement options and initiatives before making further investments.	M
Knowledge management	Using A/B testing methods to determine the effectiveness of different knowledge management, presentation, and communication techniques and tools before making further investments.	M
Organisational change management	Using A/B testing methods to determine the effectiveness of organisational changes before making further investments.	M
Problem management	Using A/B testing methods to determine the effectiveness of workarounds and error control approaches before making further investments.	M
Service validation and testing	Defining and performing service, validation, and product-testing activities using A/B testing methods.	M

5: Ensuring valuable investments

Using the ITIL 4 practice guides

A practice is *"a set of organizational resources designed for performing work or accomplishing an objective. These resources are grouped into the four dimensions of service management."*

The practice guides are hosted on the My ITIL site[26]. Anyone who takes an ITIL exam will have one year's access to My ITIL, or there are paid subscriptions available.

This publication contains all the material you need to pass the exam, but if you wish to access the practice guides for further reading during or after your studies, you will need to use the My ITIL site.

The practice guides are used to describe the 34 ITIL 4 practices and are referred to in all Specialist, Strategist and Leader publications. Additionally, selected content in the guides will contribute to the syllabuses for these courses.

ITIL® Foundation: ITIL 4 Edition provides a brief overview of each practice. The other four publications (CDS, DPI, HVIT, DSV) all refer to the guides and describe how they can be applied.

ITIL practices and ensuring valuable investments

There are two ITIL practices highlighted as important for ensuring valuable investments. We're going to review:

- Portfolio management
    - Purpose and description
    - Practice success factors (PSFs)
- Relationship management

---

[26] *www.axelos.com/my-axelos/my-itil*.

5: Ensuring valuable investments

- Purpose and description
- Practice success factors (PSFs)

Portfolio management

The purpose of the portfolio management practice is *"to ensure that the organisation has the right mix of programs, projects, products, and services to execute the organisation's strategy within its funding and resource constraints"*.

A portfolio is *"a collection of assets into which an organisation chooses to invest its resources in order to receive the best return"*.

There are several types of portfolios.

- **Product and service portfolio**
  "The complete set of products and services that are managed by the organisation, representing the organisation's commitments and investments across all of its customers and market spaces. This portfolio also represents current contractual commitments, new product and service development, and ongoing improvement plans."
- **Project portfolio**
  "Used to manage and coordinate projects, ensuring that objectives are met within time and cost constraints and to their specifications. The project portfolio also ensures that projects are not duplicated and stay within the agreed scope, and that resources are available for each project. This portfolio is used to manage single projects as well as large-scale programs. It supports the organisation's product and service portfolio and

5: Ensuring valuable investments

improvements to the organisation's practices and service value system (SVS)."

- **Customer portfolio**
  "This portfolio reflects the organisation's commitment to serving certain consumer groups and market spaces. It may influence the structure and content of the product and service portfolio and the project portfolio. The customer portfolio is used to ensure that the relationship between business outcomes, customers, and services is well understood."

> Using the Banksbest case study, map the information you have available to you into the product, project and customer portfolio perspectives. What do you know? Does the portfolio view make you look at any of the case study information differently? For example, the customer portfolio would include business clients, landlords and residential mortgage customers. Business clients and landlords have more in common; do the residential mortgage customers 'fit'?

Portfolios can be used to manage resources, including customers, applications and suppliers. Their purpose is to

5: Ensuring valuable investments

achieve optimal return on the investment and use of the assets. Figure 12[27] shows the portfolio management practice.

---

[27] *ITIL® 4: High-velocity IT*, figure 2.1. Copyright © AXELOS Limited 2020. Used under permission of AXELOS Limited. All rights reserved.

5: Ensuring valuable investments

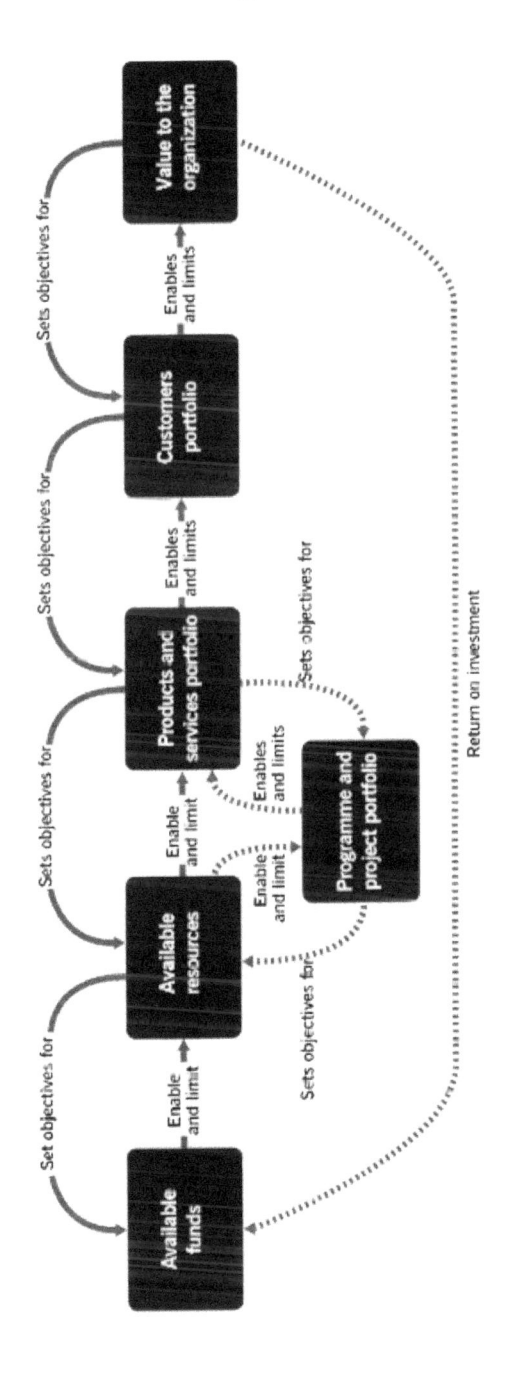

Figure 12: Portfolio Management Practice – Organisation portfolios enable return on investments

5: Ensuring valuable investments

Portfolio management is closely related to many different practices, but none more so than the service financial management practice. As portfolio management ensures fiscal management (when to invest, how to invest, etc.), costing, value propositions and other data from service financial management are crucial.

A value proposition is *"an explicit promise made by a service provider to its customers that it will deliver a particular bundle of benefits"*.

A practice success factor (PSF) is *"a complex functional component of a practice that is required for the practice to fulfil its purpose"*.

There are two PSFs for portfolio management. They are to:

- Ensure sound investment decisions for programs, projects, products and services within the organisation's resource constraints; and
- Ensure the continual monitoring, review and optimisation for the organisation's portfolios.

Table 11: Portfolio Management PSFs

PSF: Ensure Sound Investment Decisions
As organisations grow or change their focus, the many initiatives possible can create conflicting priorities. This practice ensures that the stakeholder view is included in the prioritisation activities so that more important initiatives are provided with the necessary resources before less important initiatives.
All portfolio entries are assessed against the organisational strategy, understanding the value and risk

5: Ensuring valuable investments

propositions. The assessment criteria and how they are applied should be transparent and consistent.

The financial valuation of each possible initiative is provided by the service financial management practice, and the organisational strategy is communicated by organisational leadership and the strategy management practice.

Portfolios focus on the prioritisation and reprioritisation activities of an organisation, ensuring product and service activities provide the necessary value proposition. Additionally, as portfolios get larger, there should be a named owner to ensure the necessary information is captured, updated and shared, as required.

The use of a portfolio to manage investment decisions should be clearly communicated to all decision-makers in the organisation. This keeps the method and application of prioritisation consistent and transparent.

PSF: Ensure Continual Improvement

While initiatives are prioritised based on projected value, the potential value delivery needs to be monitored and assessed against the original value proposition. If the product or service is providing the necessary value, that item remains in the portfolio. If the product or service fails to deliver the promised value, then that item needs to be improved or removed from the portfolio.

Note: products and services could deliver the necessary value proposition but no longer meet the strategic needs of the organisation. These products and services would also be removed from the portfolio.

5: Ensuring valuable investments

> The portfolio owner should review their portfolio regularly and provide a 'health check' report. This report should capture the value realised from each portfolio item. To make this simple and comparable, it is good practice to create a template and use it across all portfolios. This allows the comparison of the results of the assessment against predetermined criteria.
>
> Based on the findings from an assessment of the portfolio, new initiatives or improvement efforts are a typical outcome. The change enablement practice will provide guidance on how to manage these actions as well as during the decision to retire or remove products or services from the portfolio.

Relationship management

The purpose of the relationship management practice is *"to establish and nurture the links between the organisation and its stakeholders at strategic and tactical levels".*

To achieve this purpose, the relationship management practice establishes a culturally based, consistent approach for interaction with its stakeholders (e.g. users, customers, partners, suppliers, and others).

Cultural basis includes aspects such as:

- *"Shared or mutually recognized goals*
- *No-blame cooperation and collaboration*
- *Continuous learning*
- *Open and transparent communications*
- *Conflict prevention and mediation"*

5: Ensuring valuable investments

Stakeholder management is critical to relationship management. To be successful, think broadly about how to identify internal and external stakeholders. Beyond our users, customers, partners and suppliers, who else could be considered a stakeholder?

Consider:

- Internal teams and individual team members
- Managers
- Executives
- Auditors and other controls
- Shareholders
- Customers
- Users
- Sponsors
- Investors and shareholders
- Government and regulators
- Competitors
- Partners and suppliers
- Various social groups
- Professional communities

> Read the profile of Doug Range in the Banksbest case study. Who are his stakeholders? How would good

5: Ensuring valuable investments

> relationship management make him more effective in his role?

Any interaction in a relationship is between people. The impact of human nature and values should be remembered as each relationship is managed. Understanding the organisational cultural differences, including the type of relationship (commercial/non-commercial), level of formality, group or individual dynamics, level of professionalism, as well as the perceived hierarchy between the parties, will enhance the relationship.

There are three PSFs for relationship management:

- Establish and continually improve an effective and healthy approach to relationship management across the organisation.
- Ensure effective and healthy relationships within the organisation.
- Ensure effective and healthy relationships between the organisation and its external stakeholders.

Table 12: Relationship Management PSFs

PSF: Continually Improve the Approach

How relationships are handled in an organisation will reflect organisational values, such as openness, collaboration, no-blame and psychological safety.

Working with other practices, such as workforce and talent management, strategy management and supplier management, the relationship management practice will develop and maintain techniques that reflect these values.

How relationships are managed is strongly related to the organisational strategy as well as to how external factors (PESTLE) affect the organisation. Ensure that any behaviour rules are adopted and followed across the organisation.

PESTLE is an acronym that generically defines external factors that could affect an organisation. The acronym stands for political, economic, social, technical, legal and environmental factors.

PSF: Effective and Healthy Internal Relationships

To create effective external relationships, a strong, positive internal culture must exist. We know how important customer or user satisfaction is to the success of an organisation. Employee satisfaction is just as important.

Organisations have started to focus on protecting previously vulnerable groups (e.g. embracing diversity through diversity and inclusion initiatives), and have made greater efforts to understand and foster job and employee satisfaction. A good step is to ensure a formal assessment of internal environmental conditions occurs when there is a change in the organisational environment (such as a new strategy, a restructure, etc.).

It's important to understand the organisational climate – it will be reflected in the relationships the organisation develops. Remember that happy employees lead to happy users and customers.

PSF: Effective and Healthy External Relationships

5: Ensuring valuable investments

External relationships include customers, users and sponsors (the sponsor is the role that authorises budget for the consumption of a product or service). The obvious measurement for these service relationships is simple: customer satisfaction.

Relationship management will use appropriate techniques to ensure that needs and expectations are met and managed.

The service provider also has to manage non-service-related relationships. Non-service-related relationships that need to be managed include:

- *"Government and regulators*
- *Society and community*
- *Industry and competition*
- *Shareholders, investors, sponsors*
- *Media"*

While these groups have different interests to the product or service consumer group, these relationships still need to be actively managed. Operations will require a level of transparency, and good communication is mandatory. Other ITIL practices will be involved in these relationships, specifically portfolio management, business analysis, risk management and strategy management.

CHAPTER 6: ENSURING FAST DEVELOPMENT

There are various techniques and practices that support the HVIT objective of fast development. The techniques include:

- Infrastructure as code;
- Loosely coupled information system architecture;
- Reviews;
- Continual business analysis;
- Continuous integration/continuous delivery;
- Continuous testing; and
- Kanban.

The supporting ITIL practices for this objective include:

- Architecture management;
- Business analysis;
- Deployment management;
- Service validation and testing; and
- Software development and management.

Techniques for ensuring fast development

'Fast development' is about the quick, reliable and frequent delivery of new and improved digital products and services. Value realisation is directly tied to the speed at which digital products are delivered. In some instances, market demand might not align with early delivery. In this case, strategies must be in place in order to gain the greatest benefit from the

6: Ensuring fast development

new or improved product or service. Products and services need to be aligned with market demand.

On its own, fast development has no intrinsic value. The value rests within the product or service that is being created and released. Many organisations see a conflict between fast development and associated frequent releases when compared to the more traditional cautious approach to IT changes. Traditional thinking says that change disrupts things, therefore fewer changes decrease the risk of instability.

As the demand for change increases, a new philosophy has developed. Smaller changes reduce disruption and smaller changes mean more change is possible. By changing more frequently, the organisation now benefits from the functionality associated with the newer (and more frequent) changes. Agile and DevOps techniques embrace this philosophy. Practices have developed within these environments that are challenging the traditional view. Specifically, *"...frequency of deployment, lead time for change, and change failure rate correlates with version control, continuous delivery, and automated testing"*.

Evidence from various studies have shown that change approval, based on peer review, is no less risky than using a change advisory board.

6: Ensuring fast development

> One of the most common criticisms of ITIL is that it slows down the work that takes place in IT teams. ITIL is portrayed as bureaucratic, with the change advisory board (CAB) often cited as an example of an unnecessary blocker. It's not true to say that ITIL is an organisational blocker, but organisations do need to continually review how they do things to ensure they aren't inadvertently introducing delays or waste. We can think of the evolution of change management (now referred to as change enablement in ITIL 4) as being linked to the evolution of technology. When I was a change manager in a government organisation more than a decade ago, the CAB provided a useful purpose – allowing information to be shared between teams and risks to be assessed. There was no real way for me to automate the information sharing and discussions that took place at the CAB. If I wanted to deliver that benefit today, I could take advantage of the many advances in technology, including automated testing (to replace discussion and 'best guess' approvals), integrated delivery pipelines, automated rollback, etc.

Infrastructure as code

"Infrastructure as code (IaC) enables faster provisioning of environments, contributing to faster development and more resilient operations."

6: Ensuring fast development

Using the capabilities of the cloud, infrastructure can be created, modified and removed via remote interfaces.

The ability to manage and provision infrastructure and platforms via machine-readable definitions rather than manual configurations enables faster provisioning and better version control. IaC follows the principle of idempotence, which states that the environment will always be configured into the specified state, regardless of what the current state is.

The benefit of IaC is simple: the digitisation of infrastructure and platforms enables faster and more reliable infrastructure deployment – not only for the production environment but also the development and test environment. This can reduce wait time for teams across the product and service lifecycle, as well as ensuring consistency across environments.

When using the technique of IaC, the activities within the service value chain that will most benefit are:

- Design and transition
- Obtain/build
- Deliver and support

What ITIL practices would support IaC activities? As a hint, think about what practices are associated with the various service value chain activities and would be appropriate for this technique. Review table 13 below and pay close attention to the high-impact practices.

6: Ensuring fast development

Table 13: Practices for Which Infrastructure as Code Is Relevant[28]

ITIL management practice	Activities/resources associated with infrastructure as code	Impact
Architecture management	Verifying architectural decisions and comparing infrastructure solutions.	H
Change enablement	Enabling the fast provisioning or decommissioning of virtual infrastructure components in order to balance speed of delivery with governance, risk, and compliance needs.	H
Deployment management	Automating the deployment of infrastructure, ensuring a faster and more repeatable and reliable deployment of both infrastructure and applications.	H

---

[28] *ITIL® 4: High-velocity IT*, table 1.5. Copyright © AXELOS Limited 2020. Used under permission of AXELOS Limited. All rights reserved.

6: Ensuring fast development

Information security management	Designing and enforcing security policies in virtual infrastructure components.	H
IT asset management	Tracking the use of commercial software licences assigned to virtual infrastructure components that are often provisioned or decommissioned quickly.	H
Knowledge management	Storing virtual server configuration files and making them available for IaC automation.	H
Service configuration management	Designing and maintaining configuration management databases and relationships at the appropriate level of granularity to track virtual infrastructure components that are often provisioned or decommissioned quickly.	H
Service financial management	Shifting funding from capital expenditure to operating expenditure due	H

6: Ensuring fast development

	to reduced investment in physical infrastructure.	
Service request management	Automating the provisioning or decommissioning of virtual infrastructure components.	H
Service validation and testing	Designing and maintaining test cases to ensure that virtual IaC meets organisational requirements and policies.	H
Software development and management	Developing software architecture and code to leverage fast delivery/provisioning of virtual hardware infrastructure.	H
Incident management	Automating (where appropriate) incident recovery tasks by leveraging IaC capabilities.	M
Infrastructure and platform management	Fast delivery/provisioning of virtual hardware infrastructure.	M

6: Ensuring fast development

Problem management	Problem detection and error control leveraging IaC capabilities.	M
Service continuity management	Designing appropriate continuity plans to reflect the organisation's use of IaC capabilities.	M
Supplier management	Selecting suppliers who can provide IaC capabilities or leverage the organisation's investments in IaC.	M
Risk management	Recognizing risks introduced or mitigated through the use of IaC.	L

Loosely coupled information system architecture

Small, relatively independent elements are the foundation for a loosely coupled information system. These components allow work to be completed in small, independent product-, platform- or service-based teams. This allows each team to focus on what they know best.

With close collaboration between the teams, fast development, valuable investments, resilient operations and co-creation of value are delivered as outcomes.

Compare this with tightly coupled architectures (or even the concept of application strangulation), which have a low speed of change. In these environments, change will impact

6: Ensuring fast development

many components, causing a delay in redesign and re-release. Monolithic systems are the antithesis of loosely coupled architecture.

Two techniques, microservices and containerisation, are often used with loosely coupled architecture.

Microservices is *"a variation of the service-oriented architecture in which an application is designed and developed as a set of small, loosely coupled services, each running in its own process and using lightweight mechanisms to communicate"*.

Containerisation refers to *"the technique of packaging software into standardized lightweight, stand-alone, executable units for development, shipment, and deployment"*.

Benefits of this type of architecture include:

- Faster development, supporting more frequent change;
- Evolutionary architecture;
- Efficiency (less work needed for redesign or redeveloping); and
- Focus on products and services rather than components.

Service value chain activities that relate most with the loosely coupled information system architecture technique for fast development are:

- Plan
- Design and transition
- Obtain/build

6: Ensuring fast development

Table 14 details the ITIL practices that have great relevance to loosely coupled information system architecture. Pay close attention to the high-impact practices.

Table 14: Practices for Which Loosely Coupled Information System Architecture Is Relevant[29]

ITIL management practice	*Activities/resources associated with loosely coupled information system architecture*	*Impact*
Architecture management	*Designing loosely coupled service, technical, and information architectures.*	H
Business analysis	*Understanding consumer needs and translating them into detailed requirements for each component of a loosely coupled service architecture.*	H
Deployment management	*The scope of deployments and deployment patterns is reduced with the decoupling of system architecture; this makes deployments easier to manage and replicate, and strong candidates for automation.*	H

---

[29] *ITIL® 4: High-velocity IT*, table 4.6. Copyright © AXELOS Limited 2020. Used under permission of AXELOS Limited. All rights reserved.

6: Ensuring fast development

Information security management	*Designing and managing information security policies for loosely coupled services and service components.*	H
Infrastructure and platform management	*The detailed design, building, running, and management of loosely coupled infrastructure and platform components.*	H
Problem management	*Investigating problems and designing error controls that span multiple loosely coupled systems.*	H
Service configuration management	*Designing and maintaining information on various services and service components and their interrelationships.*	H
Service level management	*Designing and aligning service levels from a loosely coupled architecture with consumer expectations at the point of service consumption.*	H
Software development and management	*The detailed design, building, running, and management of loosely*	H

6: Ensuring fast development

	coupled software components.	
Change enablement	*Loosely coupled architecture lowers the risks associated with changes to applications and infrastructure, should those changes fail. The lower risk profile results in changes being approved at the team level, rather than at the divisional or organisational level, reducing bureaucracy.*	*M*
Incident management	*When incidents are isolated, their investigation and resolution can be planned and performed in a less stressful and more efficient way. The impact of service disruptions in loosely coupled architecture is generally constrained to the unserviceable configuration item (CI) and not the other CIs. This is due to the design principle that system components should be resilient and not depend on available services from other CIs. As a result, incidents*	*M*

6: Ensuring fast development

	have a lesser impact on customers.	
Service financial management	*Loosely coupled system architecture allows the coupling and decoupling of third-party services more easily, enabling the service provider to leverage price reduction and new offers. This flexibility also requires the service provider to employ an Agile costing accounting model to efficiently switch providers.*	M
Supplier management	*Establishing contracts and managing performance when some components of a loosely coupled architecture are provided by suppliers or external service providers.*	M
Strategy management	*Decoupling tightly coupled architecture is a strategic-level decision, due to the investment required and the potential operating model implications of taking advantage of it (e.g. introducing autonomous teams). An example of this architecture is service-*	L

6: Ensuring fast development

| | *oriented architecture that may incorporate third-party services as part of the end-to-end service.* | |

Loosely coupled architectures have many benefits. Problems that occur are contained and have a smaller impact, and new functionality can be simpler to deploy. But no technology change is free from disadvantages, and service managers need to be aware of the potential issues associated with any architectural change such as the move to a more loosely coupled architecture. Microservices can add complexity, and the links and dependencies between them must be understood and managed.

I have found on many occasions that the symptom and the cause of an IT failure can be very far apart. A small change in system A leads to a completely unexpected incident in system Z – if we don't understand how the pieces fit together, it can be hard to achieve resilient operations. You may well have seen this too with the systems that you work with.

Reviews

The ITIL principle progress iteratively with feedback includes reviews and acting on lessons learned. HVIT defines two types of reviews:

6: Ensuring fast development

- **Retrospectives**
  From Agile methodologies, a retrospective is a team meeting at the end of a sprint to discuss the efficiency and effectiveness of the iteration. This type of feedback supports fast development. Retrospectives should be scheduled regularly and be managed by a facilitator. This supports continual improvements to products and services and ways of working. Any improvement activities identified must be managed and acted on, or the review will deliver no benefit.

- **Blameless post-mortems**
  A blameless post-mortem is *"a non-judgmental description and analysis of the circumstances and events that preceded an incident"*. The criticality of incident-free operations within the digital environment is almost unmeasurable. While incident-free operation is rare, the service provider must allow teams to participate in post-mortems without fear. The focus of a blameless post-mortem is on the 'what' and not the 'who' of an incident, with the intent of understanding the cause as well as developing a plan for improvements. The results should be shared with those who would benefit (leading to transparency to co-create value and trust).

6: Ensuring fast development

> **?** Think about the last incident review or post-mortem you were involved with in your organisation. Was it free of blame? How would blame-free post-mortems change behaviour in your organisation?

For retrospectives, the service value chain activities that correlate the most are:

- Design and transition
- Obtain/build

For blameless post-mortems, the service value chain activity that correlates the most is deliver and support.

Tables 15 and 16 define the ITIL practices that strongly relate to retrospectives and blameless post-mortems. Pay close attention to the high-impact practices.

Table 15: Practices for Which Retrospectives Are Relevant[30]

ITIL management practice	Activities/resources associated with retrospectives	Impact
Continual improvement	Activities and techniques to review continual improvement	H

---

[30] *ITIL® 4: High-velocity IT*, table 4.7. Copyright © AXELOS Limited 2020. Used under permission of AXELOS Limited. All rights reserved.

6: Ensuring fast development

	initiatives periodically or upon completion, to understand whether intended outcomes are being achieved.	
Project management	*Activities and techniques to review project work and learn lessons that can benefit future similar projects.*	H
Service level management	*Activities and techniques to review and, if needed, modify service levels periodically to understand how to improve.*	H
Software development and management	*Activities and techniques to review work periodically to understand how to improve.*	H
Change enablement	*Activities and techniques to review the effectiveness and efficiency of making changes periodically to understand how to improve (including decisions on creating or suspending standard change models).*	M
Incident management	*Activities and techniques to review incident management work periodically or after*	M

6: Ensuring fast development

	major incidents to understand how to improve.	
Problem management	*Activities and techniques to review problem and error controls periodically to understand how to improve.*	*M*
Relationship management	*Activities and techniques to regularly review the status and direction of existing relationships with various stakeholders.*	*M*
Risk management	*Activities and techniques to review risk mitigations periodically, or after a mitigation has been triggered, to understand how to improve.*	*M*
Service continuity management	*Activities and techniques to review the efficiency and effectiveness of continuity plans after recovering from a disaster.*	*M*
Service desk	*Activities and techniques to review service desk interactions periodically to understand how to improve.*	*M*
Supplier management	*Activities and techniques to regularly review the status*	*M*

6: Ensuring fast development

| | and direction of existing relationships with various partners and suppliers. | |

Table 16: Practices for Which Blameless Post-mortems Are Relevant[31]

ITIL management practice	Activities/resources associated with blameless post-mortems	Impact
Change enablement	*Investigating successful and failed changes to identify opportunities to improve the success of future changes.*	H
Deployment management	*Investigating successful and failed deployments of service components to identify opportunities to improve the success of future deployments.*	H
Incident management	*Investigating incident management (and major incident management) activities to identify opportunities to improve.*	H
Problem management	*Adjusting the leadership approach to examine the*	H

---

[31] *ITIL® 4: High-velocity IT*, table 4.8. Copyright © AXELOS Limited 2020. Used under permission of AXELOS Limited. All rights reserved.

6: Ensuring fast development

	system rather than the people. Blameless post-mortems help organisations to obtain more information about the circumstances related to incidents. This provides better information for problem identification and investigation.	
Project management	*Investigating project activities to identify lessons learned and opportunities to improve future projects.*	*H*
Release management	*Investigating successful and failed releases of services to identify opportunities to improve the success of future releases.*	*H*
Continual improvement	*Investigating continual improvement activities to identify lessons learned, understand changes in the system, and identify opportunities to increase or maintain the success of future improvements.*	*M*
Information security management	*Obtaining more information about the circumstances*	*M*

6: Ensuring fast development

	related to security breaches and security incidents.	
Risk management	*Assessing risk mitigations after they have been triggered to understand how to improve mitigations and responses to current and future risks. Amending risk registers and exploring new areas of possible risks.*	M
Service desk	*Investigating engagement with external stakeholders to identify opportunities to improve interactions and ongoing communications.*	M
Service validation and testing	*Investigating successful and failed validation and testing activities to identify opportunities to improve the success of future efforts.*	M
Software development and management	*Capturing lessons learned and ideas for improvements from sprints. Involving partners and suppliers to gather feedback for the learnings register.*	M

6: Ensuring fast development

Continual business analysis

As the HVIT environment can be characterised as one that has a high degree of change by its nature, it is important to regularly elicit feedback from the user community. This can include creating feedback loops in the development cycle by using techniques such as those recommended in DevOps (reviewing each iteration) or by following a minimum viable product release with incremental releases, each improved using feedback.

A feedback loop provides information around 'next steps' so that future features meet the current needs of the user. In traditional development methodologies, feedback happens at the end of life of a version and is used to improve the next version. In this way of working, features available since the initial release may have absolutely no value, but this isn't realised because the feedback loop was too long.

Activities in the service value chain that benefit from this fast development technique include:

- Plan
- Improve
- Design and transition

Table 17 defines the ITIL practices that strongly relate to continual business analysis. Pay close attention to the high-impact practices.

6: Ensuring fast development

Table 17: Practices for Which Continual Business Analysis Is Relevant[32]

ITIL management practice	*Activities/resources associated with continual business analysis*	*Impact*
Business analysis	*Continually scanning customers, market conditions, and the broader ecosystem to understand their impacts on the organisation's products and services.*	*H*
Infrastructure and platform management	*Continually scanning customers, market conditions, and the broader ecosystem to understand their impacts on the organisation's infrastructure and platform products.*	*H*
Portfolio management	*Continually scanning customers, market conditions, and the broader ecosystem to understand their impacts on the way the organisation invests in various products and services. Monitoring*	*H*

---

[32] *ITIL® 4: High-velocity IT*, table 4.9. Copyright © AXELOS Limited 2020. Used under permission of AXELOS Limited. All rights reserved.

6: Ensuring fast development

	ongoing portfolio investments to identify value leakage or to verify value co-creation.	
Project management	*Continually scanning customers, market conditions, and the broader ecosystem to understand their impacts on the organisation's projects and associated business cases.*	*H*
Relationship management	*Continually scanning customers, market conditions, and the broader ecosystem to understand their impacts on the organisation's relationships with external stakeholders.*	*H*
Risk management	*Continually scanning internal and external corporate risks to assess and understand their impact on the organisation's products and services, and to design appropriate mitigations and countermeasures.*	*H*
Service design	*Continually scanning customers, market conditions, and the broader*	*H*

6: Ensuring fast development

	ecosystem to understand their impacts on the customers' and users' experiences of the organisation's products and services.	
Software development and management	Continually scanning customers, market conditions, and the broader ecosystem to understand their impacts on the organisation's software products and the prioritization of ongoing software development work.	H
Strategy management	Continually monitoring and evaluating customers, market conditions, and the broader ecosystem to understand their impacts on the organisation's products and services and adjust the strategy accordingly.	H
Architecture management	Continually scanning the use of technology within the organisation and by external stakeholders to understand its impacts on the organisation's technical,	M

6: Ensuring fast development

	service, and information architecture.	
Knowledge management	*Continually scanning customers, market conditions, and the broader ecosystem to create a shared understanding among relevant stakeholders.*	*M*
Service continuity management	*Continually scanning customers, market conditions, and the broader ecosystem to understand their impacts on the organisation's continuity and disaster recovery measures.*	*M*
Supplier management	*Continually scanning customers, market conditions, and the broader ecosystem to understand their impacts on the organisation's relationships with partners and suppliers.*	*M*

Continuous integration, continuous delivery and continuous deployment

Agile practices, specifically software engineering, provide three different methods for the delivery of new or changed software. These methods can also be applied to system development. The methods, collectively known as **CI/CD**, are:

Continuous integration

"An approach to integrating, building, and testing code within the software development environment."

Each time developers store changes within a central source code repository, the application to which the change applies is rebuilt and automated testing takes place. If testing fails, developers can respond quickly. At all times, the software is in a working state. (This is a type of incremental application improvement.)

Continuous delivery

"An approach to software development in which software can be released to production at any time. Frequent deployments are possible, but deployment decisions are taken case by case, usually because organisations prefer a slower rate of deployment."

Continuous delivery uses a concept of progressive deployment 'rings', with the first ring known as the 'canary release' (only accessible to the internal IT team or other relevant internal users). Each 'ring' of deployment includes wider and wider user populations.

Continuous deployment

"An approach to software development in which changes go through the pipeline and are automatically put into the production environment, enabling multiple production deployments per day. Continuous deployment relies on continuous delivery."

The goal of CI/CD is to deploy smaller changes with higher frequency. This reduces risk (by introducing less complexity

6: Ensuring fast development

with each change) and increases the velocity of value delivery (so that more useful changes are delivered more quickly to consumers).

In CI/CD the flow from development to production is optimised with a focus on removing the bottlenecks that reduce change velocity. Agile and Lean principles provide a foundation for CI/CD activities.

One additional deployment technique is the 'blue/green deployment'. The existing version and the new version run in identical production environments ('blue' and 'green', respectively). Load balancing directs a small number of users to the 'green' (new version) environment. If an incident occurs, traffic is redirected to the 'blue' (current version) version. If operation is as expected, the 'green' environment becomes the default environment.

> How could CI/CD practices support the My Way project? Consider the biometric elements, changes to cheque pay-in and the monitoring of customer feedback.

The service value chain activities that correlate most strongly with CI/CD are:

- Design and transition
- Obtain/build

6: Ensuring fast development

Table 18 defines the ITIL practices that strongly relate to CI/CD. Pay close attention to the high-impact practices.

Table 18: Practices for Which CI/CD Are Most Relevant[33]

ITIL management practice	Activities/resources associated with CI/CD	Impact
Change enablement	The rate of change to the organisation's products and services can be adjusted by using a CI/CD pipeline in line with business needs and expectations.	H
Deployment management	The systematic/automatic installation of specific versions or packages of software to a predetermined environment (integration, user acceptance testing, production).	H
Infrastructure and platform management	Use of CI/CD techniques for digital infrastructure.	H
Release management	Recognition that the deployment of software and the release of functionality	H

---

[33] *ITIL® 4: High-velocity IT*, table 4.10. Copyright © AXELOS Limited 2020. Used under permission of AXELOS Limited. All rights reserved.

6: Ensuring fast development

	are often distinct activities that help to plan and manage releases.	
Service configuration management	Managing code repositories and the associated tools that form parts of a CI/CD toolchain, and continually updating CMDB(s) to reflect when significant (CI-level) changes have been made.	H
Service validation and testing	Developing automated test cases to support continual integration activities.	H
Software development and management	Use of CI/CD techniques that are used for application software.	H
Architecture management	Designing and improving service, technical, and information architecture to leverage CI/CD capabilities. Containerization is an architectural choice that supports CI/CD.	M
Information security management	Ensuring compliance with information security policies by reducing manual work. Increasing the scale and	M

6: Ensuring fast development

	scope of automation by leveraging CI/CD tools may help to ensure compliance with information security policies by reducing manual work and improving the traceability of changes.	
Knowledge management	*Continually updating knowledge bases to ensure that the organisation maintains an up-to-date understanding of the software being built and deployed through CI/CD pipelines.*	M
Service continuity management	*CI/CD pipelines should be set up to push software components to continuity and disaster recovery systems.*	M
Risk management	*Reducing the impacts of certain types of enterprise risks through the use of CI/CD automation*	L

Continuous testing

Testing is an activity that should be performed throughout the software development lifecycle. Traditional (usually waterfall) approaches to test planning, where testing occurs

6: Ensuring fast development

just before deployment, are rarely enough. Review table 19 for different types of software testing.

Table 19: Types of Software Testing[34]

Testing the ideas	*All software originates with an idea, often an attempt to solve a problem. Testing the idea helps to determine its quality from a customer perspective (based on wants and needs) and a business perspective (based on metrics, including growth, revenue, conversion, and user base).*
Testing the artefacts	*Artefacts, such as epics, user stories, acceptance criteria, data flow diagrams, and process flow diagrams, should be tested. Inspecting the information within the artefacts can help to identify ambiguities, assumptions, and information relating to risks and variables. This information can be used as feedback to help review and improve the artefacts.*
Testing the user experience and the user interface designs	*Artefacts are used for design activities, programming activities, and testing activities. The design activities produce more design artefacts than can be tested. Interfaces and experience are*

---

[34] *ITIL® 4: High-velocity IT*, table 4.11. Copyright © AXELOS Limited 2020. Used under permission of AXELOS Limited. All rights reserved.

6: Ensuring fast development

		tested using relevant artefacts, and test results may affect other artefacts.
Testing the architecture and code designs		When designing software architecture and discussing how to build it and new features, exploratory testing can enhance the designs and ideas.
Testing the code		Code reviews are an important part of building a high-quality product. Anyone should be able to read the code and test it from different perspectives. Unit testing verifies that each unit of the software performs as it should. Unit tests are often automated. It is important to note that this is the first point within the software development lifecycle where there should be something tangible to measure against.
Testing the operational software		Testing the operational software is the most common activity that is associated with testing. Many Agile teams include 'testing' as a status within their workflow after development. However, testing should not be a status in a workflow; it should be a series of structured activities conducted throughout the software development lifecycle.

6: Ensuring fast development

Testing in different environments	*When it comes to test environments, a risk-based approach may be appropriate. There are many risks that can be tested for. Some of these cannot be tested for in a development environment. For others, a stringently integrated environment is needed for testing. Some risks can only be tested for in the real production environment.*
Testing the release pipelines	*Pipeline processes can be tested, and teams often do so implicitly in order to enhance their pipelines to be as efficient and fast as possible. This requires a good understanding of the structure behind pipeline testing.*
Testing the system in production	*Some risks must be tested for in the production environment, such as performance risks (particularly user load and user stress risks), user acceptance testing (where users use the system as they would the live software), and observability risks (to test the effectiveness of observability solutions and implementations).* *When testing in production, the aim should be to minimize the risk of testing affecting the customers. Strategies to achieve this include:* • *Canary releases*

6: Ensuring fast development

	The new feature is initially released to a small, targeted group of users, gradually increasing to all users. • Feature toggles Features can be hidden behind a feature flag, easily enabled or disabled by toggling the flag on or off. • Blue/Green deployments Two identical production environments run simultaneously (one 'blue' and one 'green'), with only one of the environments being live, serving all production traffic, whereas the other is used for deployment of the new versions. • Automated roll-back strategies Automation tools can quickly revert the release to its previous version in the event of an incident.
Testing the services in production	There are many services, activities, and technologies that are implemented for released production software, which can all be tested. From a service delivery perspective, it is important to test processes. For example, when testing whether a user can access support, it is important to ask, how easy is it for users to get

6: Ensuring fast development

> support? What opportunities do users have within the software to do that?

Continuous testing requires a number of principles to be in place and followed. They include:

- *"Tests with the fewest external dependencies should be favored.*
- *Write once, run anywhere, including in the production system.*
- *Products should be designed for testability.*
- *Test code is product code; only reliable tests survive.*
- *Testing infrastructure is a shared service.*
- *Test ownership follows product ownership.*
- *Fault injections and chaos engineering in production should be practiced to test service resilience.*
- *Unreliable tests should be eliminated."*

Attitudes to testing have changed significantly as IT organisations move from waterfall to more Agile ways of working. I've worked on many IT projects where the project manager optimistically assigned a few weeks for testing towards the end of the project timeline. As other activities slipped, testing time became contingency time, and testing activities were shortened, or perhaps didn't even happen at all. Missing out on testing can seem like a

6: Ensuring fast development

> neat way to get some time back but will usually end up with errors being deployed into the live environment. Because they affect users there, the cost and the impact to value co-creation are much higher.
>
> Seeing testing as a thread that runs through the entire lifecycle of a product elevates the importance of test activities and makes sure they aren't missed out.

Within the service value chain, these activities will benefit the most from continuous testing:

- Design and transition
- Obtain/build
- Deliver and support

Table 20 defines the ITIL practices that strongly relate to continuous testing. Pay close attention to the high-impact practices.

Table 20: Practices for Which Continuous Testing Is Most Relevant[35]

ITIL management practice	*Activities/resources associated with continuous testing*	*Impact*
Architecture management	*Designing and improving service, technical, and information architecture to leverage CI/CD capabilities.*	H

---

[35] *ITIL® 4: High-velocity IT*, table 4.12. Copyright © AXELOS Limited 2020. Used under permission of AXELOS Limited. All rights reserved.

6: Ensuring fast development

Service validation and testing	*Unit, integration, and regression testing is conducted on an ongoing basis throughout the development lifecycle. This includes application unit testing, infrastructure service testing, functional/non-functional testing, canary releases, blue/green testing, and infrastructure security testing.*	H
Deployment management	*Changes or deployments that cause the continuous testing to fail trigger the team's Andon cord. The team members then swarm to resolve the issue.*	M
Information security management	*Ensuring compliance with information security policies by reducing manual work. Leveraging automated testing tools may help to ensure compliance with information security policies by reducing manual work and improving the traceability of changes.*	M

6: Ensuring fast development

Problem management	Automated tests help to verify problem resolution, the presence of known errors, or the effectiveness of workarounds.	M
Service continuity management	Automated testing can accelerate the provisioning of technical resources needed to recover from a disaster.	M
Risk management	Reducing the impact of certain types of enterprise risks using test automation.	L

Kanban

Kanban is *"a Lean method based on a highly visualized pull-based workflow that manages and improves work across human systems by balancing demands with available capacity, and by improving the handling of system-level bottlenecks"*.

Kanban is used to develop and maintain a predictable and constant flow of work. Used properly, significant acceleration in the development of products and services is realised. Kanban, most known for Kanban board, uses a pull-based trigger, where work is pulled from one activity to the next in the value stream.

The main practices within Kanban include:

- Visualising work;
- Limiting work in progress;

6: Ensuring fast development

- Managing flow;
- Making process policies explicit;
- Implementing feedback loops;
- Improving collaboration; and
- Evolving experimentally.

Kanban meetings (part of the Kanban rhythm, or cadences) should be regular for effective communication and understanding of the project. Topics include:

- Strategy review;
- Operations review;
- Risk review;
- Service delivery review;
- Replenishment meeting; and
- Delivery planning meeting.

A basic Kanban board has columns for To Do, In Progress and Done.

- **To Do:** Kanban makes work visible. Teams can see what needs to be done and pull work when they have the capacity to do it.
- **In Progress:** work in progress, or WIP, needs to be limited to the capacity of the resources available. Too much WIP can lead to overburden. You might

experience this yourself on a personal level. Some days there seems to be so much to do, it's hard to start anything. Kanban helps to visualise and manage workflow.
- **Done:** Kanban can be used to measure velocity – the quantity of work completed in an iteration or sprint. Lead time and cycle time can be measured using the boards. Kanban doesn't have to be complex to implement. It can be as simple as sticky notes on a wall, or a whiteboard.

Kanban pulls the flow of work through a process at a manageable pace while reducing WIP. Kanban allows teams to pull work in only when they are ready for it – reducing overburden. Kanban is designed to reduce idle time and waste in a process.

Creating a Kanban board allows organisations to see their existing workflow. Time information can be added to track cycle time and lead time. Kanban is useful for managing work that is difficult to estimate and can be used to see the impact of changes on overall WIP. Kanban can be a good place to start any transformation as it is not disruptive and provides a visual of WIP.

I've found Kanban to be an incredibly powerful tool for managing my workload in both my personal and my professional life. As knowledge workers, we don't necessarily produce anything tangible, and many of my peers report feeling exhausted at the end of a busy day, but at the same time not knowing what they've accomplished. Kanban allows us to visualise what we've done.

6: Ensuring fast development

When considering the service value chain, Kanban techniques support these activities:

- Plan
- Obtain/build

Table 21 defines the ITIL practices that strongly relate to Kanban. Pay close attention to the high-impact practices.

Table 21: Practices for Which Kanban is Relevant[36]

ITIL management practice	Activities/resources associated with Kanban	Impact
Change enablement	Visualizing and improving the flow of changes to services and service components by limiting work in progress.	H
Continual improvement	Visualizing and improving the flow of improvements into the SVS.	H
Project management	Visualizing and improving the flow of work across projects and teams.	H

---

[36] *ITIL® 4: High-velocity IT*, table 4.13. Copyright © AXELOS Limited 2020. Used under permission of AXELOS Limited. All rights reserved.

6: Ensuring fast development

Release management	Visualizing and improving the quality of releases to consumers.	H
Software development and management	Visualizing and improving the flow of new or changed software components into live environments.	H
Incident management	Visualizing and improving the speed and quality of incident resolution by limiting work in progress.	M
Portfolio management	Visualizing and improving the flow of investments across the portfolio pipeline(s).	M
Problem management	Visualizing and improving problem and error control by limiting work in progress.	M
Supplier management	Visualizing supplier onboarding/offboarding progress.	M

ITIL practices and ensuring fast development

The supporting ITIL practices for ensuring fast development include:

- Architecture management;

6: Ensuring fast development

- Business analysis;
- Deployment management;
- Service validation and testing; and
- Software development and management.

Architecture management

The purpose of the architecture management practice is *"to explain the different elements that form an organisation"*.

Additionally, architecture management focuses on how the elements interrelate, enabling the organisation to effectively achieve its current and future objectives. Principles, standards and tools must be in place to effectively manage the organisation's architecture.

The layers of an organisation's architecture include:

- Business architecture;
- Product and service architecture;
- Information systems architecture;
- Technology architecture; and
- Environmental architecture.

How the organisation manages the various architectural layers will depend on the organisational strategy and vision. When determining the scope of architecture management, consider the structure of an organisation and the architectural layers that would need to be managed. For example, an internal service provider would focus on products, services, information systems and technology. Enterprise architecture would focus on the business and environmental architectures. If the business delivered products and services

6: Ensuring fast development

commercially, architecture management would focus on all layers.

What layers would an organisation manage if it had outsourced its technology to a third party? It is likely that the lower levels of technology architecture would be the responsibility of the external service provider, if it is providing the platform and infrastructure.

All four of the ITIL dimensions should be considered as well as the elements within the service value system. If these elements are considered within the architecture management practice, these objectives are achieved:

- *"The organisation's current architecture is understood and mapped to the organisation's strategy*
- *The target organisation's architecture is identified and agreed*
- *The organisation's architecture is continually optimized to achieve the target architecture"*

To meet these objectives, start by analysing the current architecture and creating a baseline model. Then, use the model to identify gaps that may hinder the achievement of the organisational strategy. Applying the strategy, a target reference model is defined. Now, the architecture can be updated and revised as the strategy and the environment change.

There are two practice success factors (PSFs) for the architecture management practice:

- *"Ensuring that organisation's strategy is supported with a target reference architecture*

6: Ensuring fast development

- *Ensuring that organisation's architecture is continually evolving to the target state."*

Table 22: Architecture Management PSFs

PSF: Target Reference Architecture
An organisation's architecture should support the organisational strategy and ensure the strategy is achievable. This is the purpose of a target reference architecture, or model. To develop a target reference model, the architect should consider the: - *"Organisation's strategy and its current performance* - *Current organisation's architecture, benefits, and constraints* - *Major pain points and their mapping to the architecture* - *Organisation's portfolios and ongoing developments* - *Environmental factors and trends* - *Technology trends, risks, and opportunities"* Analysis of this information allows the architect to understand the current and future desired state of the organisation, and then the appropriate architecture can be developed and maintained. Architecture effectiveness can be measured in a variety of ways. These might include: - Scalability - Cost-effectiveness

6: Ensuring fast development

- Compatibility with other organisations
- Compliance
- Agility
- Sustainability
- Security

Several other practices will interface with the architecture management in the achievement of the target reference model. Those practices include:

- Strategy management;
- Service design;
- Portfolio management;
- Risk management;
- Software development and management; and
- Infrastructure and platform management.

PSF: Continually Evolving Architecture

To meet this PSF, there must be an architectural roadmap, ensuring there are progressive initiatives to update the current architecture, thereby moving it closer to the target reference architecture. It is important to manage the changes as projects or programmes and ensure that stakeholders and other practices are included in the planning and execution of those plans.

A roadmap is a plan that would include *"recommendations and requirements for the taxonomy, standards, guidelines, procedures, templates, and tools , which are to be used for any architecturally important initiative"*.

6: Ensuring fast development

> Established architectural standards should be maintained as changes are deployed. This indicates that the architectural management practice must be involved in every service value stream that deploys new or changed components, new or additional third-party services, or other changes to the architecture. While the target architecture may never be achieved, architecture management shouldn't be a constraint to its evolution.

Business analysis

The purpose of the business analysis practice is to *"analyze a part or the entirety of a business, define its needs, and recommend solutions to address these needs and/or solve a business problem. The solutions must facilitate value creation for the stakeholders. Business analysis enables an organisation to communicate its needs in a meaningful way and express the rationale for change. This practice enables an organisation to design and describe solutions that enable value relation, in alignment with the organisation's objectives."*

The practice enables meaningful communication, the ability to express the reason for change, and design solutions for value creation. The needs of both the customer and the organisation are identified and addressed so an appropriate solution is deployed. Business analysis also ensures the solutions are cost-effective.

As organisations move to a more digital orientation, Agile practices become more embedded in business operations and are used outside of their roots in IT and software development. Digital organisations need a stronger tie to the strategic initiatives, customer and user experience, exploitation of technology, and business process re-

6: Ensuring fast development

evaluation, and an acceptance of digital business architecture. Working in an Agile manner, small, specialised work groups are now using the business analyst as a product or service owner. As digital solutions become more embedded in the business value stream, business analysis moves from being an intermediary to an *"integrated business practice"*.

> Business analysis has been an established role for many years, with comprehensive training programmes and publications available. Do some research in your own organisation to see if business analysis capabilities already exist – you may be able to leverage them as part of your service management endeavours. Agile business analysis practices are also growing to reflect the move to more Agile ways of working.

Two PSFs have been defined for the business analysis practice:

- *"Establish and continually improve an organisation-wide approach to business analysis to ensure that it is conducted in a consistent and effective manner*
- *Ensure that current and future needs of the organisation and its customers are understood, analyzed, and supported with timely, efficient, and effective solution proposals."*

6: Ensuring fast development

Table 23: Business Analysis PSFs

PSF: Establish and Continually Improve an Organisation-wide Approach to Business Analysis
Consistency is vital within the business analysis practice, but consistency doesn't mean that every task needs to be performed in exactly the same manner. The context of the task will dictate the model that is required. For example, consider the difference between an Agile environment and a traditional waterfall approach. Business analysis is a 'thoughtful' practice – tasks include the objective analysis of information for wise business investments. Skills include data modelling, analysing organisational structure, processes, scope and decision making.
PSF: Ensure Current and Future Needs are Understood
Business analysis translates ideas into solutions. Not only do ideas need to be communicated clearly but also the recipient must have the steps necessary to deploy the idea. Ideas are communicated with two intents: - Customers needing a solution to fulfil a need, typically via business case. - Service provider's teams that design, develop and deliver the solution, based on documented requirements, recommendations and priorities. The skills needed for good business analysis include emotional intelligence and service empathy.

6: Ensuring fast development

Deployment management

The purpose of the deployment management practice is *"...to move new or changed hardware, software, documentation, processes, or any other component to live environments. It may also be involved in deploying components to other environments for testing or staging."*

Compare this to release management, which ensures services are available for use; deployment performs the actual task of moving the 'release' to a designated environment.

A release is *"a version of a service or any other configuration item, or a collection of configuration items that is made available for use"*.

Agile practices, specifically software engineering, provide three different methods for the delivery of new or changed software. These methods can also be applied to system development. The methods (we defined them earlier – they are collectively known as CI/CD) are:

- Continuous integration
- Continuous delivery
- Continuous deployment

The goal of CI/CD is to deploy smaller changes with higher frequency. This reduces risk (through less complexity) and increases the velocity of value delivery (more useful changes delivered more quickly to consumers).

In addition to deployment management, practices that support CI/CD activities include:

- Software development and management;
- Service validation and testing;
- Infrastructure and platform management; and

145

6: Ensuring fast development

- Release management.

These practices require specific skills, processes, procedures and automation tools to enable the pipeline of continuous integration, delivery and deployment. These activities would affect the activities of additional practices, such as service configuration management, monitoring and event management, incident management, and others.

> Deployment is where the 'rubber hits the road'. Get things wrong here, and all of your careful planning to date can be wasted. I've seen deployment issues in organisations where there are poor relationships between teams; this is where ways of working like DevOps can add real benefit by making sure there are good relationships between teams and effective communication takes place.

The two PSFs for deployment management mirror the PSFs for release management:

- *"Developing a consistent approach to the deployment of products and services*
- *Ensuring the release of products and services effectively integrate with the organisational value streams."*

6: Ensuring fast development

Table 24: Deployment Management PSFs

PSF: Consistent Approach to Deployment

The use of deployment models ensures consistency in deployment activities. Deployment models are based on several factors including automation, frequency, rate of change, source of components, and visibility of the change. Each deployment model should also define the flow of activity through the target environment, roles and responsibilities, triggers, and interfaces with other practices.

One of the processes defined within the deployment management practice is the development of deployment models. These models can describe the practice itself, review of already developed models, and deployment procedures.

Deployment models should be reviewed regularly (at least quarterly), and reviews may also be triggered by a failed deployment. Review figure 13[37] for the overall process for deployment models.

---

[37] *ITIL® 4: Deployment Management Practice Guide*, figure 3.3. Copyright © AXELOS Limited 2020. Used under permission of AXELOS Limited. All rights reserved.

6: Ensuring fast development

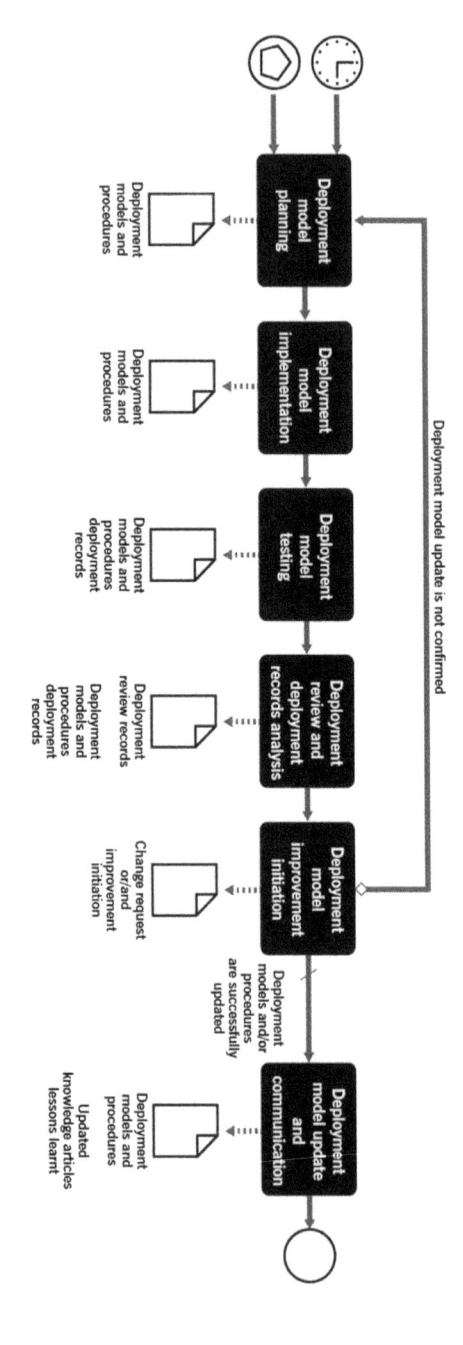

Figure 13: Deployment Management – Workflow of the deployment model's development and review process

6: Ensuring fast development

Example deployment models for service components are shown in table 25.

Table 25: Example Models for The Deployment of Different Service Components[38]

Deployment model applicability	Organizations and people	Information and technology	Value streams and processes	Partners and suppliers
Hardware components of services provided to external service consumers	A service provider should arrange a delivery team for the transportation and installation of the components	A range of tools can be used to automate the procurement, invoicing, user communication, and scheduling of the installation of hardware	An installation order can be triggered by new or changed value streams that include clear authorizations to procure and install new hardware	Third-party shipping, delivery, and installation service providers can be employed, as agreed between the parties
Hardware components of services obtained from a vendor	According to the delivery and installation clause in the vendor	Vendor catalogues may be used for ordering the components,	Vendor activities, such as invoicing and shipping,	

---

[38] *ITIL® 4: Deployment Management Practice Guide*, table 2.1. Copyright © AXELOS Limited 2020. Used under permission of AXELOS Limited. All rights reserved.

6: Ensuring fast development

Deployment model applicability	Organizations and people	Information and technology	Value streams and processes	Partners and suppliers
	contract, the responsibilities for obtaining hardware and ensuring its correct installation should be clearly defined	as well as to store and provide up-to-date installation manuals. A configuration management tool should be populated with documentation supplied with the hardware, including records and documents, such as warranty certificates, maintenance schedules, and so on	should be accounted for during the value stream design; interfaces between parties need to be founded in the contracts	
Software components of service provided to external service consumers	The service provider can have staff perform roadshows to service consumers to promote new	An automated deployment toolset is utilized to make software available	Service providers can implement additional controls before a component	Partners can be engaged in deployment, such as additional bespoke

6: Ensuring fast development

Deployment model applicability	Organizations and people	Information and technology	Value streams and processes	Partners and suppliers
	software components and facilitate change awareness	for use or ordering	is deployed, such as quality assurance, security, or comercial; is crucial to account for such controls in partially or fully automated deployment pipelines	testing of the software made available by the vendor prior to its deployment to the consumer environment.
Software components of service developed in house	DevOps teams are likely to perform the deployment of software	The continual integration and continual deployment pipeline toolset can be used to deploy software to a controlled environment	Service provider organisations have to establish organisational controls over the course of deployment, ensuring that controls	Third parties can action some steps of the deployment model; for example, manual environment configuration activities

6: Ensuring fast development

Deployment model applicability	Organizations and people	Information and technology	Value streams and processes	Partners and suppliers
			are not excessive	

Table 26: Deployment Management PSFs

PSF: Effective Integration of Products, Services and Value Streams
To ensure effective deployments, changes and releases must be strictly managed. Component integrity is crucial – there should be no unauthorised activity to the change or release during the deployment practice. The effectiveness and efficiency of a deployment depends on the availability of resources, skills, technology, tools and infrastructure. The use of automation improves the deployment practice through better consistency, removal of manual error, and efficiency.

Service validation and testing

The purpose of the service validation and testing practice is *"to ensure that new or changed products and services meet defined requirements"*.

As a reminder, *"the definition of service value is based on input from customers, business objectives, and regulatory requirements and is documented as part of the design and transition value chain activity. These inputs are used to*

6: Ensuring fast development

establish measurable quality and performance indicators that support the definition of assurance criteria and testing requirements."

The activities of service validation and testing have the goal of reducing the introduction of risks and uncertainties into the live environment as new or changed products and services are deployed. Testing every possibility is usually impossible due to cost and time constraints. The level of testing needs to be clearly defined based on:

- *"Agreed requirements that a service or product must meet*
- *Impact and likelihood of deviations from the agreed requirements"*

Understanding the requirements with respect to possible deviations allows for informed testing and ensures that testing takes place in the areas where the deviations are most likely.

Service validation takes place early in the lifecycle (including during ideation and design) and its purpose is to confirm the design will meet the agreed requirements. Service validation also establishes acceptance criteria for the next stages (development, deployment and release).

Testing is based on the criteria from the validation activities. Test strategies and test plans are developed and implemented. Test plans are based on the defined test strategies.

A test strategy *"defines an overall approach to testing and can be applied to environments, platforms, sets of services or individual products or services"*. A test plan *"defines the detailed activities, estimates, and schedules for each test phase (levels of testing)".*

Today's digital environment requires a holistic focus, including velocity, security, agility and stability. Service validation and testing needs to reflect these characteristics. This is achieved through a close integration with the following practices:

- Architecture management
- Software development and management
- Project management
- Infrastructure and platform management
- Release management
- Deployment management
- Incident management
- Problem management

Don't forget the roles and their collaborative work: testers, developers and operations teams need to work together to formulate the appropriate tests and correctly interpret results.

There are two PSFs for service validation and testing:

- *"Defining and agreeing an approach to the validation and testing of the organisation's products, services, and components in line with the organisation's requirements for speed and quality of service changes.*
- *Ensuring that new and changed components, products, and services meet agreed criteria."*

6: Ensuring fast development

Table 27: Service Validation and Testing PSFs

PSF: Define and Agree Approaches to Validation and Testing
Service validation and testing should develop an approach to capture the utility and warranty requirements for any product, service or component. Gather this information from: • *"Stakeholders (customer and user requirements and feedback)* • *Business requirements* • *Compliance and regulatory requirements* • *Security and risk controls"* These requirements should then be translated into acceptance criteria for the product or service.
PSF: Ensure New and Changed Components Meet Agreed Criteria
"Ensuring that new and changed components, products, and services meet agreed criteria" is the second PSF for service validation and testing. It is within this PSF that a large proportion of the work is completed. To achieve this outcome, the test strategy is critical. A test strategy is created for each project and is tailored to the project outcomes. There are several elements that should be defined and managed when considering the test strategy. They include:

6: Ensuring fast development

- **Test organisation** – separate testers from developers to remove any possible bias.
- **Test planning and control** – match the testing methodology with the development methodology (e.g. involve testing in each iteration or increment if following an Agile approach), the type of system/service (e.g. testing a financial system where the system has different requirements throughout the year when compared to an online shopping site) and fully considering the activities around the application elements (e.g. consider data migration, training, operational readiness, release management practices, reporting, etc.).
- **Test analysis and design** – report on the progress of testing with a full understanding of the test schedule (what has been done and what remains) before drawing any conclusions of success or failure of the test results.
- **Phases and cycles** – consider the order of tests when planning (e.g. test new features first as they tend to have the highest risk of negative impact).
- **Test preparation and execution** – provision the test environment carefully and protect the test data so that when the tests are executed, the results are indicative of the prepared environment and no other factors.
- **Evaluating exit criteria and reporting** – know when to stop! Previously defined acceptance (exit) criteria define 'good enough' and testing stops at this

6: Ensuring fast development

> point. Tests that have failed should be reported and corrective action taken.
>
> - **Test closure** – this stage can trigger early life support (ELS) activities, the release of test resources and archiving of test assets (including strategies, plans, reports, scripts), and provides an opportunity to capture lessons learned for continual improvement.

Software development and management

The purpose of software development and management is *"to ensure that applications meet internal and external stakeholder needs, in terms of functionality, reliability, maintainability, compliance, and auditability"*.

While this practice primarily focuses on application software, the principles are also applicable to infrastructure software (e.g. firmware). Infrastructure management and platform management have direct ties to software development and management. Consider the HVIT practice of infrastructure as code – in this practice, hardware components are configured with machine-readable files to accurately and quickly provision IT infrastructure and platforms.

Software development and management is applied to the entire lifecycle of an application. The lifecycle of an application can be anything from a few months to more than 15 years. In High-velocity organisations, a majority of the total cost of application ownership moves to development – in an Agile world, delivering the next iteration of the application is seen as a development cost and not part of the costs assigned to maintenance/operations.

6: Ensuring fast development

Software development and management will coordinate with service design to ensure the smooth transition of any developed applications to support a new product or service.

> How could effective software development and management practices improve the reputation of some of the live IT services at Banksbest? Take a look at Bizbank and Mortbank and think about what Banksbest could do to improve the situation for those services, and to make sure the issues don't arise for any new services.

There are eight software development and management terms that you need to understand.

1. **Software**: software is a set of instructions that tell the physical components (hardware) of a computer how to work. Software manifests itself in applications for end users but also in the underlying infrastructure that is needed to develop and operate applications. Software and infrastructure are service components that are combined with other service components or resources to form products and services.

2. **Software development**: software development is the design and construction of applications according to functional and non-functional requirements, and the correction and enhancement of operational applications

according to changing functional and non-functional requirements.

3. **Maintenance**: maintenance includes the modification of an application as part of development and use, for both correction and enhancement purposes:

- **Corrective**: correcting defects in the application that have caused incidents.
- **Preventive**: preventing defects in the application before they have manifested themselves.
- **Adaptive**: adapting the application to work with changed infrastructure.
- **Perfective**: enhancing the functionality, usability and performance of the application (sometimes known as 'additive maintenance', 'enhancement' or 'development').

4. **Software quality**: software quality provides a qualification of the value of software as a product and in its use. A common categorisation (based on ISO/IEC 25010:2011) is:

- **Product quality:** functional suitability, performance efficiency, compatibility, usability, reliability, security, maintainability and portability.
- **Quality in use:** effectiveness, efficiency, satisfaction, freedom from risk, and context coverage.

5. **Technical debt**: technical debt describes the total rework backlog accumulated by choosing workarounds

instead of system solutions. In the case of software development and management, it includes the total amount of rework needed to repair substandard (changes to) software.

6. **Software Development Lifecycle (SDLC) Model**: The SDLC model describes the sequence in which the stages of the software development lifecycle are executed. The major stages are:

   - Establish requirements
   - Design
   - Code
   - Test
   - Run/use the application

   Different models can be applied to the SDLC:

   - Waterfall model: each stage of the development lifecycle is executed in sequence, resulting in a single delivery of the whole application for use.
   - Incremental model: after the requirements and priorities for the whole application have been established, the application is developed in parts (builds). For each build, each of the further stages of the development lifecycle is executed in sequence. Builds can be (partially) developed in parallel, and the application is delivered in useable parts.
   - Iterative or evolutionary model: after the requirements and priorities for the whole application have been partially established, the application is developed in separate builds such as in the

6: Ensuring fast development

incremental model, but because the requirements could not be fully established at the start, the design, coding, testing or use of a build may lead to refinement of the requirements, leading to refinement of part of the application in another build.

7. **Scrum**: Scrum is an iterative, timeboxed approach to product delivery that is described as "a framework within which people can address complex adaptive problems, while productively and creatively delivering products of the highest possible value."[39]
8. **Definition of done**: This is the agreed criteria for a proposed product or service, reflecting functional and non-functional requirements.

Software development and management has two PSFs:

- *"Agree and improve an organisational approach to development and management of software*
- *Ensure that software continually meets organisation's requirements and quality criteria throughout its lifecycle"*

This practice focuses on an organisation-wide application of the practice activities. There is also a focus on the quality and value of the practice outcomes. What should be noted is the concept of models in this practice – software development and management advocates that there can be several models or approaches to accommodate the different types of

---

[39] *The Scrum Guide* (2017) by Ken Schwaber and Jeff Sutherland.

6: Ensuring fast development

products and services. The approach used will depend on the customer requirements and organisational objectives.

Table 28: Software Development and Management PSFs

PSF: Agree and Improve an Organisational Approach to Software Development and Management

A number of approaches have been described to develop and manage software. While not all the defined methods are required at any one organisation, the competencies to deploy new or changed software following multiple approaches should be available.

This is a strategic decision for the organisation, and it will affect a number of practices, including:

- Architecture management
- Business analysis
- Change enablement
- Release management
- Deployment management
- Information security management
- Portfolio management
- Risk management
- Service validation and testing
- Strategy management

Software development and management will determine which approach is best based on the software product, and the consumer and the organisational requirements.

In addition to the practices that will be affected by the strategic approach to software development and

6: Ensuring fast development

management, two additional practices will engage in order to realise this PSF:

- **Continual improvement practice:** requirements for software development and management emerge from organisational performance information and other improvement activities, which in turn are documented as improvement initiatives and plans.
- **Organisational change management practice:** as the plans for improvement are executed, OCM will engage to ensure the changes are incorporated in software development and management work practices.

PSF: Ensure that Software Continually Meets Requirements

There are many ways to describe software quality – quality could be focused on the product itself (e.g. suitability, compatibility, usability, etc.) or its use (e.g. effectiveness, satisfaction, efficiency, etc.).

There is an international standard, ISO/IEC 25010:2011 – *Systems and software engineering — Systems and software Quality Requirements and Evaluation (SQuaRE) — System and software quality models*, that defines both models (product use and product quality). Within this document, the steps and/or objectives necessary to develop or revise software products are provided.

The elements that are critical to the achievement of this PSF include:

6: Ensuring fast development

- *"Understanding the source code, how the various modules are interrelated, and the application architecture*
- *Understanding the requirements and the context in which the application is used*
- *Ensuring that non-functional (warranty) requirements are included in the definition of done*
- *Creating tests before coding*
- *Effective version control of all application artefacts*
- *Approaching the task of coding with a full appreciation of its tremendous difficulty and respecting the intrinsic limitations of the human mind*
- *Adhering to coding conventions*
- *Peer review*
- *Fast feedback from testing, for example by using automated testing, and taking remedial action quickly"*

In addition to the above elements, the following practices would also be involved:

- Business analysis
- Service validation and testing
- Infrastructure and platform management
- Problem management

CHAPTER 7: ENSURING RESILIENT OPERATIONS

There are various techniques and practices that support the HVIT objective of resilient operations. The techniques include:

- Technical debt
- Chaos engineering
- Definition of done
- Version control
- AIOps
- ChatOps
- Site reliability engineering (SRE)

The supporting ITIL practices for this objective include:

- Availability management;
- Capacity and performance management;
- Monitoring and event management;
- Problem management;
- Service continuity management; and
- Infrastructure and platform management.

Techniques for ensuring resilient operations

The purpose of resilient operations is to ensure the digital product or service is available whenever needed. Value from a product or service is only realised when the product or service is available. There is no value in the specific components per se, the value is only realised with use and the fulfilment of a specific need.

7: Ensuring resilient operations

Resilience doesn't add value but allows the potential value to be realised. There is a change of emphasis from increasing the time between failures to a quick restoration of service, thus minimising disruption. Resilient services are now the expectation of any service consumer. The use of cloud technology and the 'always on' mentality underpin this expectation. Resilient services are measured in a range of ways including availability, performance and security.

Availability is traditionally measured as a percentage representing uptime. It can also be a specific metric of 'mean time between failures' and 'mean time to restore service'. **Performance** can be measured in a variety of ways; typically, how long does it take to do something? **Security** measures can include the number of security breaches (these can be hard to measure – are you sure you captured all of them?), the maturity of the controls in place, and the ability to analyse log information to help identify risks and potential/actual breaches.

Technical debt

From the software development and management perspective, technical debt is defined as *"the total rework backlog accumulated by choosing workarounds instead of system solutions that would take longer"*.

As software is used, issues occur and enhancements to the original software are needed. The actions of fixing or enhancing applications tend to degrade the quality of the original software even as more functionality is added. The code being used may not be as 'elegant' as the original, meaning not as concise or as efficient, thus causing the overall code to slow down. This is known as ***software entropy***.

7: Ensuring resilient operations

When the focus is on restoring service or rolling out enhancements as quickly as possible, developers don't always have time to see what is wrong or how the fix integrates with the original code. Expediency may overcome good practice – using a quick fix (workaround) or pasting in a solution because the issue has been resolved and the product or service is once again functional. Every time a workaround is applied without full consideration of its long-term impact and supportability, technical debt increases. There is, however, a fine line when discussing technical debt – it can be perfectly acceptable to have level of debt…as long as it is NOT prohibitive.

Individual organisations will make cost–risk decisions when dealing with technical debt. The important thing is to ensure that the level of technical debt building up is understood, rather than just allowing it to grow over time until the situation becomes unsustainable.

When considering the concept of technical debt to achieve resilient operations, the activities within the service value chain that will most benefit are:

- Design and transition
- Obtain/build
- Improve

Which ITIL practices support the management of technical debt? Review table 29, paying close attention to the high-impact practices.

7: Ensuring resilient operations

Table 29: Practices for Which Technical Debt Is Relevant[40]

ITIL management practice	*Activities/resources associated with technical debt*	*Impact*
Incident management	Incident resolution and management requires knowledge of existing technical debt and the efforts planned to resolve it.	H
Infrastructure and platform management	Identifying and reducing technical debt by creating or modifying infrastructure and platform service components.	H
Knowledge management	Ensuring that all relevant stakeholders have access to up-to-date information.	H
Portfolio management	Deciding whether to invest resources to fix the technical debt present in live products and services and understanding the	H

---

[40] *ITIL® 4: High-velocity IT*, table 4.14. Copyright © AXELOS Limited 2020. Used under permission of AXELOS Limited. All rights reserved.

7: Ensuring resilient operations

	impact on investments towards future products and services.	
	Assessing technical debt so that new portfolio items can be introduced to the existing pool.	
	Assessing the technical debt of current portfolio items to prevent value drain.	
Problem management	*Applying problem control and error control methods to manage technical debt.*	H
Software development and management	*Identifying and reducing technical debt by creating or modifying infrastructure and platform service components*	H
Business analysis	*Understanding the impact of technical debt on the articulation of requirements and solutions.*	M

7: Ensuring resilient operations

Continual improvement	*Identifying, prioritizing, and managing efforts to reduce technical debt.*	*M*
Information security management	*The design, implementation, and improvement of information security controls are influenced by existing technical debt. Information security controls can also result in the creation of technical debt, which needs to be acknowledged and communicated to all relevant stakeholders.*	*M*
Project management	*Planning and executing projects is influenced by existing technical debt.* *Projects can also result in the creation of technical debt, which needs to be acknowledged and communicated to all relevant stakeholders.*	*M*
Risk management	*Recognizing the impact of technical debt on new*	*M*

7: Ensuring resilient operations

	or existing enterprise risks; risk mitigations may create technical debt that needs to be acknowledged and communicated to all relevant stakeholders.	
Service desk	Communicating with external users who need assistance with incidents and requests requires knowledge of existing technical debt and efforts planned to resolve it.	M

Chaos engineering

Chaos engineering is defined as *"the discipline of experimenting on a system in order to build confidence in the system's capability to withstand turbulent conditions in production"*.

Chaos engineering tries to find events/activities (variables) that will disrupt the normal behaviour of a system and then ensure that the system has the necessary design to mitigate or overcome those events.

To run chaos engineering principles effectively, consider these activities:

- *"Build and hypothesize around steady state behavior*
- *Vary real-world events*
- *Run experiments in production*

7: Ensuring resilient operations

- *Automate experiments to run continuously*
- *Minimize the blast radius"*

The main tool that is used in chaos engineering is from Netflix®'s Simian Army – the 'Chaos Monkey'. This tool disables various components within a system to see how the system reacts. While Chaos Monkey disrupts operations in the short term, the long-term benefit is system resilience.

Chaos Monkey is *"a tool that tests the resilience of IT systems by intentionally disabling components in production to test how remaining systems respond to the outage"*. Simian Army is s suite of tools that includes several 'monkeys':

- Latency Monkey (simulates artificial delays to see how the system responds).
- Doctor Monkey (performs system health checks and shuts down unhealthy components).
- Security Monkey (finds/terminates security violations/vulnerabilities).
- Janitor Monkey (removes clutter/waste from the cloud environment).

Chaos engineering sounds terrifying, but it can deliver huge improvements. As teams and systems become more accustomed to reacting to failures, the impact of incidents

7: Ensuring resilient operations

> and the time to recover from them will decrease. Think of it like going to the gym – you build up muscles that can reduce your likelihood of injury in the future. If you've ever had to try to resolve a real issue with no clue where to start, you will see the benefit of testing and refining your approach to failures.

When considering the concept of chaos engineering to achieve resilient operations, the activities within the service value chain that will most benefit are:

- Design and transition
- Obtain/build
- Deliver and support
- Improve

What ITIL practices would support the concept of chaos engineering? Review table 30, paying close attention to the high-impact practices.

Table 30: Practices for Which Chaos Engineering is Relevant[41]

ITIL management practice	*Activities/resources associated with chaos engineering*	*Impact*
Continual improvement	Using chaos engineering as one of the most effective	H

---

[41] *ITIL® 4: High-velocity IT*, table 4.15. Copyright © AXELOS Limited 2020. Used under permission of AXELOS Limited. All rights reserved.

7: Ensuring resilient operations

	tools for improving service quality.	
Infrastructure and platform management	*Designing infrastructure and platforms for sufficient resilience and redundancy to deal with the unexpected outages caused by chaos engineering tools.* *Providing information for chaos engineering regarding service components and backup activities.*	H
Service continuity management	*Designing service continuity measures with sufficient resilience and redundancy to cope with the unexpected outages caused by chaos engineering tools.* *Continually monitoring continuity plans, measures, and mechanisms for resilience.*	H
Service level management	*Tests must be designed and run considering business continuity strategy, service level agreements, and clear criteria established for service degradation in case*	H

7: Ensuring resilient operations

	an artificial disruption exceeds acceptable levels.	
Software development and management	*Chaos engineering tools are themselves software applications that need to be developed (or configured) and managed. Software should be designed and architected with sufficient resilience and redundancy.*	*H*
Architecture management	*The building of resilient infrastructure, which is promoted by chaos engineering.* *Considering interactions between services and components in order to support demand.*	*M*
Capacity and performance management	*When running this type of test, performance information should be captured. As a result, improvements should be identified that will ensure services are designed for optimum performance, scalability, and capacity.*	*M*

7: Ensuring resilient operations

Incident management	Teams can practise responding to and recovering from outages by using chaos engineering tools. They must be prepared to manage incidents without impacting users. Redundancy and automation should be built into the processes.	M
Measurement and reporting	Chaos engineering tests involve experiments and hypotheses and will help to collect and analyse data for planning and forecasting. The results support continuity business strategy.	M
Monitoring and event management	Monitoring and event management tools can be set up to flag outages orchestrated by chaos engineering tools, or to monitor the quality of service rather than the technical components.	M
Organisational change management	Chaos engineering will help to ensure engagement and cooperation in the live environment.	M

7: Ensuring resilient operations

Problem management	*Proactively detecting problems by introducing random failures and looking for potential flaws in services/components. The data gathered from chaos engineering tools can help to identify underlying problems that require investigation and remediation.*	M
Service configuration management	*CMDBs and code repositories should have high availability and accurate information (aligned with the recovery point objectives defined by service continuity management) to help the organisation recover quickly from outages.*	M
Service design	*Chaos engineering testing principles can help architects design more resilient systems and improve user experience.*	M
Service desk	*The service desk team must be informed about the test and prepared for managing*	M

7: Ensuring resilient operations

	incidents without impacting users.	
Service validation and testing	*Chaos engineering testing principles can help to evaluate service reliability. Architects should focus on service interruption.*	M
Risk management	*Certain types of organisational risks can be mitigated by using chaos engineering tools and methods to increase organisational resilience and robustness.*	L

Definition of done

When is something 'done'? ITIL defines done as *"…a checklist of the agreed criteria for a proposed product or service"*.

Done can mean many things, but, simply, it is when the agreed functional criteria have been met and the non-functional criteria support the agreed warranty. 'Done' is when the consumer achieves their desired outcomes from their investment. When defining done, view the environment holistically with a focus on value.

Non-functional criteria typically specify the quality required for those who operate, maintain and/or enhance the system. These criteria will include availability, capacity, efficiency, maintainability, performance, privacy, reliability, recoverability and security.

7: Ensuring resilient operations

> What does 'done' mean in the product-based environment? When teams work with a product through its whole lifecycle, we need to think of 'done' as an incremental concept. We have reached a certain state of 'done' when we have an MVP to share with our customers, and another 'done' when a product or service is live, and another 'done' when we have incorporated feedback or made improvements. Until the product or service is retired, 'done' is a moving concept. From a purely Agile perspective, 'done' means having a potentially releasable product at the end of a sprint.
>
> The most important thing you need to be sure of is that everyone has the same understanding of 'done', and you are able to measure whether 'done' has been achieved. The ITIL practices in the table below explain some of the ways that service management can help to articulate and track 'done'.

When considering the definition of done to achieve resilient operations, the activities within the service value chain that will most benefit are:

- Plan
- Design and transition
- Obtain/build
- Improve

7: Ensuring resilient operations

What ITIL practices would support the definition of done? Review table 31, paying close attention to the high-impact practices.

Table 31: Practices for Which the Definition of Done Is Relevant[42]

ITIL management practice	Activities/resources associated with definition of done	Impact
Availability management	*Detailed warranty requirements for the new or changed service should be negotiated and agreed with stakeholders.*	H
Capacity and performance management	*A definition of done checklist must consider capacity requirements, demand forecasting, and performance for managing business and customer expectations.*	H
Change enablement	*Change enablement activities can be structured around a definition of done; for example, to create a boundary with release*	H

---

[42] *ITIL® 4: High-velocity IT*, table 4.16. Copyright © AXELOS Limited 2020. Used under permission of AXELOS Limited. All rights reserved.

180

7: Ensuring resilient operations

	management or deployment management.	
Continual improvement	The definition of done can be used to scope and structure continual improvement activities, and to check whether outcomes have been achieved.	H
Deployment management	Deployment management activities can be structured around a definition of done; for example, to create a boundary with release management. When moving releases to live environments, teams should verify that deliverables for support are complete: all requirements, user stories, and tests should be accepted.	H
Incident management	Incident management activities can be structured around a definition of done; for example, to create a boundary with problem management.	H
Information security management	Security tests such as vulnerability, penetration, or policy compliance should be	H

7: Ensuring resilient operations

	considered in the definition of done for resilient products and services.	
Project management	*Project tasks or outputs can define success or completion criteria using a definition of done approach.*	*H*
Release management	*Release management activities can be structured around a definition of done; for example, to create a boundary with change enablement or deployment management. The releases must be designed to match with business, customer, and user expectations. It is important to measure every release to verify that it fulfils user stories and requirements.*	*H*
Service level management	*A definition of done can articulate service actions for providers and consumers and can be used as the basis for monitoring actual performance against expected performance.*	*H*

7: Ensuring resilient operations

Service request management	*Service request management activities, such as logging or fulfilling requests, can be structured using a definition of done approach.*	H
Service validation and testing	*Testing activities can be structured around a definition of done to ensure that multiple types of tests are conducted.*	H
Software development and management	*Software can be developed (or configured) to meet a definition of done before it is deployed into live environments, ensuring that code is understandable, maintainable, and ready to support future changes.*	H
Business analysis	*Functional and non-functional requirements for warranty and utility must be captured in order to fulfil customers' needs and expectations.*	M
Service design	*The definition of done should be customer-centric, in order to make design methods easier to adopt and ensure that services will be*	M

7: Ensuring resilient operations

	maintainable and cost-effective.	
Service catalogue management	When the new functionality, product, or service is released, the service catalogue must be updated.	L
Service desk	Quality attributes are specified in the definition of done so that the development and support teams can consider them in early phases.	L

Version control

Good version control is a well-known method of achieving and supporting High-velocity IT. With good version control, change lead times can be shorter, there are more frequent deployments, and organisations experience faster service restoration times. Version control tracks not only source code but also the system components used to deliver the product or service.

Information tracked when following version control techniques includes:

- Current and previous state of every component;
- Changes;
- Date/time of a change;
- Person who made the change; and
- Other supporting information.

7: Ensuring resilient operations

There are several benefits of version control. They include:

- Support of infrastructure as code techniques;
- Quicker lead times for change, more frequent deployments, faster service restoration;
- Automated testing (supports quicker changes); and
- Supports continuous delivery (more frequent deployments).

> What version control mechanisms exist in your organisation? Have you ever seen an incident occur because of poor version control? We usually think of application increments and version control together, but poor version control for elements such as documents and knowledge articles can also have a negative effect.

When considering version control techniques to achieve resilient operations, the activities within the service value chain that will most benefit are:

- Design and transition
- Obtain/build
- Deliver and support
- Improve

What ITIL practices would support version control? Review table 32, paying close attention to the high-impact practices.

7: Ensuring resilient operations

Table 32: Practices for Which Version Control is Relevant[43]

ITIL management practice	Activities/resources associated with version control	Impact
Deployment management	Using version-controlled repositories to deploy new or changed service components or return to a previous version.	H
Information security management	Addressing or closing information security risks by flagging vulnerable versions of service components.	H
Infrastructure and platform management	Infrastructure components, configuration settings, and virtual and physical infrastructure components can be formally stored and managed using a version-controlled repository.	H
Service configuration management	CMDBs can be federated, leveraging version-controlled code repositories, infrastructure-as-code	H

---

[43] *ITIL® 4: High-velocity IT*, table 4.17. Copyright © AXELOS Limited 2020. Used under permission of AXELOS Limited. All rights reserved.

7: Ensuring resilient operations

	configuration files, and even a store of physical devices and other hardware. Check-ins should occur multiple times each day, and environment specifications should be managed and versioned.	
Software development and management	Code, and even configuration settings for other software components, can be formally managed using a version-controlled repository to house the outputs of software development and management work.	H
Continual improvement	Creating a baseline of the current environment, and updating the baseline once improvements have been made.	M
Incident management	Using a version-controlled repository of software or hardware components to resolve an incident.	M
Knowledge management	Updating knowledge repositories and communicating information	M

7: Ensuring resilient operations

	when versions of service components change.	
Service continuity management	*Understanding the impact of new versions of service components; and, if viable, propagating them into service continuity and disaster recovery plans.*	M
Service request management	*Using a version-controlled repository of software or hardware components to quickly fulfil requests.*	M

AIOps

ITIL 4 defines AIOps as *"the application of machine learning and big data to IT operations to receive continuous insights which provide continuous fixes and improvements via automation. Also referred to as 'artificial intelligence for IT operations' or 'algorithmic IT operations'."*

As the demands for velocity, flexibility and security continue to dominate the product and service industries, the method in which we manage infrastructures must change. Human capacity to perform the multitude of tasks to support this demand is diminishing. So, how can technologies help to perform these tasks?

Just as it sounds, AIOps is the combination of artificial intelligence (AI) and Operations. The AIOps platform can manage operational functions, such as availability and performance monitoring, failure recognition, predictive analysis, and event correlation and analysis.

7: Ensuring resilient operations

Using machine learning (ML), many types of data (e.g. observational, engagement) are used to 'teach' the platform what to look for and how to respond. Areas that can be managed include:

- Issue detection and prediction;
- Proactive maintenance and tuning; and
- Threshold analysis.

AIOps can be used beyond IT, allowing business managers to get real-time information about the impact of IT on the business.

> Most of the organisations I work with are at the very start of their AI implementations. AI helps their support agents to answer queries, and gives customers access to FAQs and knowledge articles, but the overall adoption of AI is still fairly limited. Expectations of AI are often higher than the results that are delivered, and the effort required is not well understood.
>
> I expect this to change more rapidly as AI becomes standardised in service management tools and use cases are more readily available. It's definitely an area where service management practitioners need to stay on top of the research and new developments to help identify opportunities to reduce waste and free up resources for more valuable work. Site reliability engineering (SRE) refers to 'toil' – repetitive, predictable tasks that scale as a

7: Ensuring resilient operations

> service grows but add little enduring value (in past times, things like changing backup tapes). These are ideal candidates for the application of automation and AI capabilities.

When including AIOps techniques to achieve resilient operations, the activities within the service value chain that will most benefit are:

- Deliver and support
- Improve

What ITIL practices would support AIOps? Review table 33, paying close attention to the high-impact practices.

Table 33: Practices for Which AIOps Is Relevant[44]

ITIL management practice	*Activities/resources associated with AIOps*	*Impact*
Capacity and performance management	*AIOps provides capabilities for identifying patterns and anomalies, determining the capacity and utilization of assets, and planning the capacity of future products or services.*	*H*
Incident management	*Incident management data can benefit from the highly*	*H*

---

[44] *ITIL® 4: High-velocity IT*, table 4.18. Copyright © AXELOS Limited 2020. Used under permission of AXELOS Limited. All rights reserved.

7: Ensuring resilient operations

	automated capabilities provided by AIOps tools that augment manual work. *Resolving correlating incidents with contextual pre-analysed data merged from different systems.*	
Infrastructure and platform management	*AIOps tools can automate much of the day-to-day management of infrastructure and platform resources.*	H
Monitoring and event management	*AIOps tools can help to correlate vast data sets from across multiple monitoring tools. They create a better understanding of the IT environment.* *AIOps enables value co-creation through an integrated set of business and operational metrics, thereby reducing the frequency of operational events or incidents because they are predicted and prevented.* *AIOps helps to optimize IT and reduce IT costs by replacing silo-focused IT monitoring tools, and by monitoring the health and performance of*	H

7: Ensuring resilient operations

	applications of all tiers in value streams.	
Change enablement	AIOPs supports the visualization of dependency details at every device level.	M
IT asset management	AIOps may collect dynamic inventory information with logical and physical attributes.	M
Measurement and reporting	AIOps provides data for metrics to evaluate performance and regulatory compliance. It also helps to automate the reporting task.	M
Problem management	Information from AIOps tools can aid in identifying and investigating problems and errors, and in automating and monitoring the application of workarounds. They can also help with proactive problem detection based on pre-processed and merged data.	M
Service configuration management	AIOps data can be used to detect changes to configuration items, helping to identify unauthorized changes.	M

7: Ensuring resilient operations

Service desk	*Information from AIOps tools can support engagement with external stakeholders. AIOps helps organisations to proactively plan, identifying issues and their business impacts before they occur. AIOps also enables the informed triage of user queries based on merged data and identified trends.*	M
Workforce and talent management	*Organisations that implement AIOps breakdown silos across their IT teams enable less-experienced staff to be more productive, developing skills and efficiencies.*	M
Knowledge management	*The combination of knowledge of IT processes, operations, performance results, and data processing algorithms supports critical business functions.*	L

ChatOps

ChatOps is a model in which *"people, tools, process, and automation are connected in a transparent flow"*. Put simply, it is an integration of instant communication and operations.

7: Ensuring resilient operations

Pioneered by the DevOps community, tools and platforms join the 'conversation' via bots. When bots are used, they can receive requests for information and fulfil that request instantly, which reduces response time, enabling High-velocity IT. ChatOps promotes feedback, improves communication and enhances team collaboration. Do you see several of the ITIL guiding principles in this technique?

> It's well recognised that silos cause harm in organisations. Collaboration tools can also unwittingly create silos, with one team working away in Slack, another in the service management toolset, and another using emails to share information. Applying ChatOps thinking helps to integrate these information silos. For example, one organisation I spoke to uses a bot to add an update to Slack whenever a change request is created in the organisation's service management toolset, increasing visibility across teams.

When including ChatOps techniques to achieve resilient operations, the activities within the service value chain that will most benefit are:

- Engage
- Deliver and support

What ITIL practices would support ChatOps? Review table 34, paying close attention to the high-impact practices.

7: Ensuring resilient operations

Table 34: Practices for Which ChatOps Is Relevant[45]

ITIL management practice	*Activities/resources associated with ChatOps*	*Impact*
Service desk	*Communicating and coordinating with users to better manage incidents and requests.*	*H*
Change enablement	*Communicating and coordinating between all teams involved in managing changes to services and service components. Some ChatOps tools can integrate with other IT and service management tools. ChatOps provides a channel for communicating with users and team members about new or changed services, thereby humanizing the way of working.*	*M*
Continual improvement	*Meeting goals of continual improvement initiatives to improve communication and coordination between teams.*	*M*

---

[45] *ITIL® 4: High-velocity IT*, table 4.19. Copyright © AXELOS Limited 2020. Used under permission of AXELOS Limited. All rights reserved.

7: Ensuring resilient operations

Deployment management	*Communicating and coordinating between all teams involved in deploying new or changed service components. Some ChatOps tools can integrate with deployment tools.*	*M*
Incident management	*Communicating and coordinating between external stakeholders and various teams involved with incident management activities. Some ChatOps tools can integrate with other IT and service management tools. ChatOps helps IT teams in support activities, such as registering, analysing, and diagnosing, thereby reducing response times and eliminating repetitive tasks.*	*M*

Site reliability engineering

Site reliability engineering (SRE) applies a software development approach to IT operations, which strengthens the alignment between development and operations. To accomplish this, SRE teams work in both areas – they execute operational tasks as well as developing software that is resilient and performance enhancing.

SRE teams work at a 'high' level – their efforts require advanced skills and capabilities. Additionally, their work

7: Ensuring resilient operations

> wish, whereas teams that have spent their budget may be subjected to extra controls. I love this idea, and it's a strong incentive for Dev and Ops to continue to work closely together.

When including SRE techniques to achieve resilient operations, the activities within the service value chain that will most benefit are:

- Design and transition
- Obtain/build
- Deliver and support

What ITIL practices would support SRE? Review table 35, paying close attention to the high-impact practices.

Table 35: Practices for Which SRE is Relevant[46]

ITIL management practice	Activities/resources associated with SRE	Impact
Availability management	*Using SRE techniques and tooling to improve visibility of a system in order to judge the service health and diagnose issues.* *Tracking the 'technical' MTBF and (more crucially) MTRS metrics, such as user outage*	H

---

[46] *ITIL® 4: High-velocity IT*, table 4.20. Copyright © AXELOS Limited 2020. Used under permission of AXELOS Limited. All rights reserved.

7: Ensuring resilient operations

	minutes, number of lost transactions, lost business value, and user satisfaction. Using error budgets to balance service reliability and innovation.	
Capacity and performance management	Using SRE techniques and tooling to improve visibility of a system in order to judge the service health and diagnose issues. Monitoring systems and defined SLOs must be accounted for and measured. Improving monitoring in order to better understand the system when things go wrong.	H
Change enablement	Using SRE techniques and tooling to enable changes to service components and the roll-back of failed changes.	H
Incident management	Using SRE techniques and tooling to manage incidents in the infrastructure or platform layers.	H
Infrastructure and platform management	Using SRE techniques and tooling to help architect and design infrastructure and	H

7: Ensuring resilient operations

focuses on preventing or reducing the impact of failure. Based on the premise that today's systems are complex and will fail, failure is viewed as a learning opportunity. With this attitude, the development of knowledge is paramount. Their work would not be defined as 'toil'. Toil is work that is manual, automatable, repetitive and tactical (rather than strategic), and doesn't have enduring or permanent value. Toil scales in a linear way, i.e. in proportion to size, volume or count.

ITIL 4 defines SRE as *"a discipline that incorporates aspects of software engineering and applies them to infrastructure and operations problems with the goal of creating ultra-scalable and highly reliable software systems"*.

With this ongoing and continuously developing 'learning system', the recognition of potential failures increases the resilient nature of the systems. One key point: SRE teams push the boundaries of risk – not to be reckless but due to the fact that there is a high level of uncertainty in the outcomes of their work. SRE teams will not be able to work effectively in an organisation with a strong blame culture.

A key 'tool' for the SRE team is an error budget. An error budget is *"a control mechanism that allocates appropriate capacity to development work for stability, ensuring the right balance between stability and new features"*. An error budget is calculated as

100% - SLO

where SLO is the service level objective. A 99.8% SLO service states the error budget is 0.2%, and those funds should be used to increase stability.

7: Ensuring resilient operations

I've been working with ITIL for more than 20 years now. When the DevOps movement gained popularity in the UK, I went to some DevOps meet-ups to talk about how ITIL and DevOps could work together. I'd seen lots of organisations where DevOps was seen as in conflict with traditional ITSM. I remember at one meet-up, talking to some DevOps practitioners who had no service desk, no incident management, and no concept of logging or sharing information about changes. It struck me at the time that ITSM needs DevOps, but some DevOps organisations also need ITSM. Site reliability engineering I find fascinating because it feels like a new flavour of ITSM has come from the DevOps community. SRE doesn't replace ITSM, but applying software engineering thinking to IT operations can provide a fresh way of looking at services, and can again help to build those relationships between development and operations.

SRE applies software development thinking to operations. Originating in Google and now being widely adopted, SRE contains some concepts that will be recognisable and of interest to service managers. For example, services are given service level agreement targets – very old-school ITSM. But what's different in SRE is that the unavailability element of the target (say the 0.1% of a 99.9% availability) is then available to the development teams as an 'error budget'. Development teams that are within their error budget can release as and when they

7: Ensuring resilient operations

	platform capabilities to meet the organisation's needs.	
Monitoring and event management	Using SRE techniques and tooling to improve visibility of a system in order to judge the service health and diagnose issues.	H
Problem management	Data from SRE tools can help to identify problems, ensuring workarounds are applied quickly through the use of automation. Automating IT processes improves resilience and reduces toil. Use of post-mortems.	H
Service design	SRE collaboration during the design phase can prevent a variety of problems or incidents from occurring later in production. Although design decisions can be reversed or rectified later in the development lifecycle, such changes come at a high cost in terms of effort and complexity.	H
Software development	Providing requirements to SRE teams and acting on feedback.	H

7: Ensuring resilient operations

and management		
Deployment management	The deployment process should align with the risk process described in service design.	M
Organisational change management	An SRE team has a core responsibility to prepare its teams for rapid innovation.	M
Release management	With SRE, techniques used for releasing software are applied to digitized infrastructure.	M
Service configuration management	With SRE, automated discovery and version control can be applied to infrastructure components.	M
Service validation and testing	For release engineering in SRE, it is recommended that continuous build test targets correspond to the same test targets that gate the project release.	M

ITIL practices and ensuring resilient operations

The supporting ITIL practices for ensuring resilient operations include:

- Availability management;
- Capacity and performance management;

7: Ensuring resilient operations

- Monitoring and event management;
- Problem management;
- Service continuity management; and
- Infrastructure and platform management.

Availability management

Availability is *"the ability of an IT service or other configuration item to perform its agreed function when required"*. The purpose of the availability management practice is to *"ensure that services deliver the agreed levels of availability to meet the needs of customers and users"*.

From a practical view, this means that the availability requirements must meet the agreed levels with the customer, but also the service provider's strategy and its commitments. Availability is crucial to planning and design activities and it is the characteristic that is most visible to the user and customer. It's what the customer negotiates for and receives information about in service reviews and reports. Simply, availability defines whether the service could be used in agreed ways by authorised users.

To measure availability, there are some straightforward indicators:

- **MTBF** – mean time between failure (MTBF) measures how frequently a service fails.
- **MTRS** – mean time to restore service (MTRS) measures how quickly a service can be restored after a failure.

But are these measures truly what availability is all about? In fact, availability is much more complex – it is a function of the service architecture, the efficiency of the various components, the agreed service hours, and how

7: Ensuring resilient operations

unavailability has been defined. When defining availability, it is best to understand the impact of the service loss to the overall operations of the business and design availability to ensure those needs are met.

Consider a seasonal service such as online sales. The ability to order is crucial at all times but more so around Christmas. The service requires high availability, where failure is mitigated by design, using techniques such as redundancy, clustering and failover.

Redundancy describes a service design that duplicates critical components so that if one component fails, the redundant component can continue delivering the service. **Clustering** is a design technique where multiple components, typically servers, are linked and work together to improve performance and/or availability of a single server. **Failover** is a design technique where critical service resources run on a primary module and a backup module runs non-critical resources, but it can handle the critical services of the primary if a fault occurs.

Think about the most critical product or service that your organisation provides, or one that you use every day. What does unavailability look like for that service? Is it straightforward (it's up, or it's down), or are there other ways to look at availability? For example, at Banksbest,

7: Ensuring resilient operations

> what happens if My Way is available, but the biometric login has failed?

The availability management practice includes three practice success factors:

- *"Identifying service availability requirements.*
- *Measuring, assessing, and reporting service availability.*
- *Treating service availability risks."*

Table 36: Availability Management PSFs

PSF: Identifying Service Availability Requirements
Identifying requirements is a critical activity within the availability management practice. Not only does the design team need to understand what the customer is trying to accomplish but they should also understand how the service will be used, the impact of an outage, and how service unavailability will be defined. ITIL defines three areas within identifying requirements. • **Understanding customer requirements** The business analysis and service level management practices typically communicate with customers to understand their availability requirements. Availability management will provide support and input to ensure those requirements can actually be met and provide more detail around quality and cost. • **Determining availability criteria**

7: Ensuring resilient operations

> The organisation should clearly define 'unavailability' so availability can actually be measured. There are several criteria in determining availability:
> - *"The criticality of business functions that are enabled by a service*
> - *Thresholds for underperformance and complete unavailability (there may be acceptable delays that should not be considered service unavailability)*
> - *Scale factor (number of users, business units, sites impacted)*
> - *Certain users, business units, sites, and so on that are impacted*
> - *The service delivery schedule and peak hours"*
>
> - **Determining availability metrics and setting targets**
>   Remember that availability is the most 'noticeable' of all service characteristics – the service needs to be 'up' for the customer to use it and fulfil their needs. Defined metrics and targets should reflect service criticality and the impact of unavailability.

PSF: Measure, Assess, Report Service Availability

The ability to provide quantifiable data about service performance and availability is critical to the service provider – it is the evidence that the service did (or didn't) meet the agreed requirements. While availability is typically represented as a percentage (e.g. 99% available),

7: Ensuring resilient operations

this isn't a great measure in terms of representing the business impact of that one percentage of downtime.

Typical methods of measuring, assessing and reporting availability include:

- Mean time between failure (MTBF);
- Minimum time between failures;
- Number of service disruptions;
- Total downtime over a period of time;
- Maximum single outage; and
- Mean time to restore service (MTRS).

Remember, whatever metrics are used, we need to reflect the business impact of unavailability, rather than just measuring components.

Where can we capture availability data? One common source is incident records – a service isn't functioning as needed. While this might be easy to capture, the accuracy and reliability of the information can be varied.

Enterprise monitoring tools provide the most reliable data, but it can be hard to show the relationship between the availability of the components and overall business operations. Use methods such as business transaction monitoring or real user monitoring (which captures server-side data to reconstruct end-user experience, or directly monitor user interactions with an application user experience at the point of service consumption) to provide a more business-oriented measure.

PSF: Treating Service Availability Risks

7: Ensuring resilient operations

> The availability management practice has been presented as critical to the service design practice, but it is also critical in risk prevention. Availability techniques make a significant contribution to risk management.
>
> Consider the four dimensions of service management. How can the availability management practice address risks? Review table 37 for some additional ideas.

Table 37: The Four Dimensions of Availability Management[47]

Service management dimension	*Countermeasures to availability risks*
Organisations and people	Developing people's capabilities with training
Information and technology	• The exploitation of fault-tolerant technology to mask the impacts of planned or unplanned component downtime • Duplexing, or the provision of alternative IT infrastructure components, to allow one component to take over the work of another component

---

[47] *ITIL® 4 Availability Management Practice Guide* table 2.4. Copyright © AXELOS Limited 2020. Used under permission of AXELOS Limited. All rights reserved.

7: Ensuring resilient operations

	• Improving component reliability by enhancing testing regimes • Improving software design and development • Introducing a resilient telecommunication network • Data protection in operation: RAID arrays and disk mirroring for LAN servers to prevent data loss and ensure the continued availability of data • Monitoring (to provide prompt alerts)
Partners and suppliers	*Improved externally supplied services, contracts, or agreements*
Value streams and processes	• *Improved incident management* • *Improved testing* • *Continuous integrations/continuous delivery*

Understanding the effectiveness and efficiency of the availability techniques is critical when considering the design of a service or risk mitigation methods.

Effectiveness describes *"the effects of availability controls should be assessed and compared to the expected losses due to incidents"*. Efficiency relates to *"the costs of an availability control should also be assessed and compared to its benefits"*.

Remember it is cheaper to have the 'right' design or level of controls from the start, rather than trying to retroactively add it later. Once a service has earned a reputation for poor availability, it can be hard to restore customer faith in it.

'Poor' service can be measured at many different levels. Consider productivity losses, fines, loss of competitive advantage, or a damaged reputation. All of these can point to a lack of availability, but all affect the customer and service provider differently. Understand also that losses will change over time – some losses may grow exponentially, while others may create such an untenable position that the provider is no longer viable.

Availability controls should be considered in service design, software development and management, and infrastructure and platform management practices. When considering risk management, availability practices should be considered with service continuity management, capacity and performance management, and information security management practices.

Capacity and performance management

The capacity and performance management practice is usually very technically oriented. It manages the performance of the service and its individual elements (e.g. applications, infrastructure, third-party services, humans). Its aim is to optimise each element to create the best-performing service possible within the agreed requirements. ITIL defines the purpose of this practice as *"to ensure that services achieve the agreed and expected levels of performance and satisfy current and future demand in a cost-effective way"*.

The activities within the capacity and performance management practice ensure 'the right amount of capacity, at the right time, with all elements cost-justified'. Note that

7: Ensuring resilient operations

this practice also considers humans as well as technology and their role in service performance.

To achieve its purpose, the practice is applied throughout the product and service lifecycle and within the scope of the organisation's strategy and commitments.

This practice underpins several other activities within service delivery, namely:

- Service availability
- Continuity
- Information security

Remember that this practice is about resources and how they are used. If you don't have capacity, how can you promise availability or continuity, or guarantee information security? You need the resources from capacity.

> Capacity isn't as much of an issue with cloud-based services as it used to be for ITSM practitioners. Rather than having strict rules about things like mailbox sizes, organisations usually have the option to just 'buy more space' as it's needed. But this also brings a new set of management issues that need to be understood. For example, if you have development teams that can create new environments, do you have policies in place about how the environments are shut down once the work is completed? Running out of capacity can cause obvious

7: Ensuring resilient operations

> service issues, but having too much capacity is also a source of waste (and unnecessary cost) that needs to be addressed.

The capacity and performance management practice include three practice success factors (PSFs):

- *"Identifying service capacity and performance requirements.*
- *Measuring, assessing, and reporting service performance and capacity.*
- *Treating service performance and capacity risks."*

Table 38: Capacity and Performance Management PSFs

PSF: Identifying Service Capacity and Performance Requirements
Customer requirements are typically captured by the service level management and/or business analysis practices. Capacity and performance management principles also need to be included in this activity. Consider the following scenarios: • Capacity and performance management will work with service level management and business analysis to ensure the requirements are feasible and then ensure the resulting service design will meet the requirements cost-effectively. • Determine performance and capacity criteria – including high and low performance criteria (this is similar to the work done to define availability

7: Ensuring resilient operations

criteria). When creating those definitions, ensure they reflect overall business functionality and not just component performance.

- Define capacity and performance metrics that illustrate the impact of service degradation to customers and users.

PSF: Measure, Assess, Report Service Performance and Capacity

Typical measures for service performance tend to revolve around the number of transactions in a time period. While this measure may have meaning for some, it's not one that is reflective of the business impact of service degradation. When developing measurements, consider the following:

- Ensure there is sufficient capacity and performance monitoring.
- Be able to translate monitoring data into service performance data.

In a similar way to the availability management practice, incident records can be a source of data for capacity and performance management. Again, the accuracy of user-reported incidents makes it difficult to directly equate this data to service performance metrics. Real-time monitoring data from infrastructure monitoring tools is useful but rarely accurately measures the performance of service actions (remember that a service will be the accumulated effect of the various components). Real user monitoring and business transaction monitoring can overcome these issues.

7: Ensuring resilient operations

> **PSF: Treating Service Performance and Capacity Risks**
>
> Capacity and performance management activities go beyond planning and monitoring performance. They also have an impact on risk mitigation. The practices that would be involved with risk mitigation include availability management, service continuity management and information security management.
>
> The risk management practice will also interface with capacity and performance management. How does this practice ensure effective risk management? Consider these areas:
>
> - *"Assessing the impacts of components' capacity and performance on the end-to-end performance of products and services and identifying related vulnerabilities and constraints*
> - *Assessing the impacts of products' and services' capacity and performance on the user and customer experience*
> - *Designing effective controls and countermeasures to prevent, detect, and mitigate capacity and performance risks*
> - *Monitoring and controlling capacity and performance risks on an ongoing basis and optimizing risk management activities within the scope of the practice."*

Monitoring and event management

The purpose of monitoring and event management is *"to systematically observe services and service components, and*

7: Ensuring resilient operations

record and report selected changes of state identified as events".

The activities of this practice include identification and categorisation (including analysis) of events throughout the infrastructure and between a service and its customers.

This practice has two elements:

- **Monitoring** focuses on services and their components to detect changes of state that have significance. This information is communicated to relevant parties.
- **Event management** manages the identified events from monitoring activities and initiates the correct response to the event.

An event is *"any change of state that has significance for the management of a service or other configuration item (CI)"*. A configuration item is *"any component that needs to be managed in order to deliver an IT service"*. Monitoring is *"repeated observation of a system, practice, process, service, or other entity to detect events and to ensure that the current status is known"*.

Monitoring proactively observes designated services and service components and reports any changes of state (or alerts) as an event. Alerts are defined by predetermining thresholds for the monitored components that when breached, will trigger a response. The action taken will depend on the classification of the event. Typical categories, in order of increasing significance, are informational, warning and exception.

A **threshold** is the defined value that triggers a response. This can lead to an **alert** that a threshold has been reached, or there is a change or a failure.

7: Ensuring resilient operations

Informational events supply information only and do not require action (for example, a backup has completed).

Warning events may require action to be taken to avoid negative impact (for example, the backup has reached 95% of the possible size).

Exception events require action to be taken and often indicate a failure or loss of performance (the backup failed to complete in time).

There are three PSFs for monitoring and event management. They are to:

- *"Establish and maintain approaches/models that describe the various types of events and monitoring capabilities needed to detect them*
- *Ensure that timely, relevant, and sufficient monitoring data is available to relevant stakeholders*
- *Ensure that events are detected, interpreted, and if needed acted upon as quickly as possible."*

Table 39: Monitoring and Event Management PSFs

PSF: Establish and Maintain Approaches and Models
Monitoring and event management has a significant challenge within its activities: data collection. There is a risk of collecting too much data, which must be factored into the practice approach and models. The intention should be to collect just enough meaningful information to support the service management activities across the organisation. To accomplish this PSF:

7: Ensuring resilient operations

- *"Identify and prioritize services and the components that are monitored. This decision is based on the business objectives and the dependency of the components to achieve them.*
- *Balance the need for information, the granularity of the data, and the frequency it is collected. The more data that is collected, the less information will be produced if only due to the amount of data collected and the effort required to filter and analyze the data. Automation and machine learning are useful tools to deploy for data analysis."*

Each organisation will need to maintain an appropriate level of technology to collect, analyse, report on and store monitored data. They should define polices to address different types of events and their associated responses as part of this practice.

PSF: Ensure the Availability of Timely, Relevant Data

Data that is relevant and timely allows effective, fact-based decisions and actions. This ability is critical for the delivery of high-quality services (including meeting service performance requirements) and continual improvement activities (including identification of underperforming areas).

Data must be available to any relevant stakeholders. For example, data from monitoring and event management can answer these stakeholder questions:

7: Ensuring resilient operations

- Service provider – is the service performing as designed? Data can benchmark the service against the design specifications.
- Customer – am I getting what I paid for? Data here will show if the performance has met (or not met) agreed service levels.
- Customer and service provider – who's at fault when something goes wrong? Data can show where the customer is causing service faults and there is a need for training, rather than a technical fix.

PSF: Detecting and Acting on Events

The last PSF for this practice focuses on the efficiency of detecting events and then acting on them. The methods within monitoring and event management can be clearly defined, but if the architecture design and/or age of the components are overly complex or not compatible with modern monitoring tools, then this practice will not provide the benefit it should.

Monitoring and event management is heavily dependent on technology. Organisations can exploit the capabilities of technological advances – for example allowing them to use automation, artificial intelligence and machine learning to reduce the need for manual collection, analysis and reporting.

Problem management

The purpose of problem management is *"to reduce the likelihood and impact of incidents by identifying actual and potential causes of incidents and managing workarounds and known errors"*.

7: Ensuring resilient operations

With any service, perfection is rare, and incidents will occur. While the incident management practice will manage individual incidents, the problem management practice will manage the **cause** of the incident. A problem is *"a cause, or potential cause, of one or more incidents"*.

> At Banksbest, Bizbank incidents can take a long time to resolve because 'the original developers have left, and documentation is poor'. Think about this situation from the perspective of a problem manager. How might you discover the problem exists? What solutions might apply? Are there any solutions that seem more appropriate than others?

There are two PSFs for the problem management practice, which are to:

- *"Identify and understand the problems and their impact on services"*
- *"Optimize problem resolution and mitigation."*

Table 40: Problem Management PSFs

PSF: Identify and Understand Problems and their Impact
When organisations understand the errors in their products and services, incidents can be mitigated or even prevented.

7: Ensuring resilient operations

> Problem management includes problem identification, contributing to the continual improvement of products and services.

PSF: Optimize Problem Resolution and Mitigation

> Once problems are identified, they need to be managed appropriately. Not all problems can be removed (or need to be removed). Problem resolution needs to balance costs, risks, and the impact of the problem on service quality.

Service continuity management

Service continuity relates to mitigating the risk of a disaster. When this practice is included in the service design and ongoing management of services, the service provider is ensuring an agreed level of service will be delivered regardless of the circumstances. The purpose of the service continuity management practice is *"...to ensure that the availability and performance of a service are maintained at sufficient levels in case of a disaster. The practice provides a framework for building organisational resilience with the capability of producing an effective response that safeguards the interests of key stakeholders and the organisation's reputation, brand, and value-creating activities."*

A disaster is *"a sudden unplanned event that causes great damage or serious loss to an organisation. To be classified as a disaster, the event must match certain business-impact criteria that are predefined by the organisation."*

This practice ensures service resilience and demonstrates that the service provider is prepared for a disaster. The conditions in which this practice operates go beyond incident management.

7: Ensuring resilient operations

The events that service continuity will address are those that aren't under the organisation's control, like natural disasters, brownouts/blackouts and catastrophic failures. Service continuity is similar to the availability management practice. Both are about good design and mitigating risk. Where they differ is in the circumstances each practice prepares for: availability is for 'normal' operations and continuity is about the 'disaster' situation. The final design from availability will be an input to continuity – if the organisation has to use a continuity environment, its design needs to match the 'normal' infrastructure.

Service continuity activities should support the corporate-level business continuity management practice.

Service continuity management is one of the group of practices that includes risk mitigation activities. We've looked at the availability management and capacity and performance management practices, and in an upcoming chapter, we will explore the information security management practice. These four practices have risk mitigation embedded in their activities. The risk management practice defined in ITIL 4 also by its nature includes risk mitigation.

Organisations all over the world have learned hard lessons about service continuity and business resilience in 2020. As I write this chapter here in the UK, six months after the global COVID-19 pandemic started, there are still

7: Ensuring resilient operations

> organisations in all industries experiencing significant issues trying to provide their normal services. The rapid move to remote working for office staff tested many continuity plans to their limits, and levels of demand from customers fluctuated wildly. Organisations that have put time and thought into service continuity planning have generally done better, but even they may not have predicted a scenario quite like this.
>
> The conversation in continuity circles is moving towards agile continuity. Rather than focusing on a perfect plan for each type of possible scenario, agile continuity will build a resilient organisation with staff who have the autonomy and empowerment to react to situations as they happen.

What other practices will ensure service resilience and demonstrate readiness for a disaster? Consider the following practices:

- Risk management
- Service design
- Relationship management
- Architecture management
- Supplier management

The service continuity management practice includes three PSFs:

- *"Developing and managing service continuity plans.*
- *Mitigating service continuity risks.*
- *Ensuring awareness and readiness."*

7: *Ensuring resilient operations*

Table 41: Service Continuity Management PSFs

PSF: Developing and Managing Service Continuity Plans
A plan is the most important element of service continuity; it allows the provider to effectively respond to and recover from a disaster. However, the plan by itself is just a start – it requires practice. The strategy chosen by the service provider should reflect customer requirements as well as the provider's capabilities. These are defined in a business impact analysis (BIA). BIA is a *"key activity in the practice of service continuity management that identifies vital business functions (VBFs) and their dependencies. These dependencies may include suppliers, people, other business processes, and IT services. Business impact analysis defines the recovery requirements for IT services. These requirements include recovery time objectives (RTOs), recovery point objectives (RPOs), and minimum target service levels for each IT service."* The Business Continuity Institute (BCI) defines several types of continuity strategies, including: - Diversification - Replication - Standby - Post-incident acquisition - Do nothing - Subcontracting

7: Ensuring resilient operations

These strategies are not one-time activities, but rather, like any plan, they should be reviewed regularly to ensure consumer and provider needs are being fulfilled by the chosen strategy.

Continuity plans should cover three levels:

- **Strategic** – *"How executives make decisions about the recovery process, communicate with external parties (including media, if relevant), and deal with any situations that are not covered in service continuity plans"*
- **Tactical** – *"How management coordinates the recovery process in order to ensure the appropriate allocation of resources according to priorities (current business priorities, seasonal changes, and so on) and manage conflicts between the planning and recovery teams"*
- **Operational** – *"How teams perform recovery activities, including responding to disruptive events, recovering to pre-defined levels of service, and/or providing alternative facilities to continue operations"*

The plans for internal service providers, whether large or small, as well as for external service providers will vary based on scale and complexity. There are typically three phases within the plan: response, recover and restore (return to normal). Regardless, the plan and supporting procedures are tested, reviewed and improved over time.

PSF: Mitigating Service Continuity Risks

7: Ensuring resilient operations

Along with the other risk-focused practices (availability, capacity, information security, risk management), the service continuity management practice will define controls to manage risks. The four dimensions can be used to devise those controls. Consider the following:

- **Organisations and People**
    - *"Managing people during disasters*
    - *Using alternative sites and facilities"*
- **Information and Technology**
    - *"Physical security*
    - *Resilient telecommunication network*
    - *Data protection in operation: using RAID arrays, SAN, and so on to ensure the availability of data*
    - *Data backup*
    - *Fault-tolerant applications*
    - *Monitoring to provide prompt alerts"*
- **Partners and Suppliers**
    - *"Reciprocal agreements*
    - *Outsourcing services to multiple providers*
    - *Fire detection systems or suppression systems as a service"*
- **Processes and Value streams**
    - *"Manual operations and alternative methods of service delivery*
    - *Plans and procedures for response and recovery (service continuity plans)"*

Remember that when choosing controls, service providers still need to apply the concepts of effectiveness and efficiency.

7: Ensuring resilient operations

> **PSF: Ensuring Awareness and Readiness**
>
> Plans are important; testing them is even more so. Testing fulfils these purposes:
>
> - Confirms the plan and procedures or discovers flaws and/or inefficiencies.
> - Acts as training for the staff involved, especially if staff rotate regularly to different teams and roles.
>
> Testing should occur regularly (the higher the possibility of an outage, the more frequent the testing) and after any significant change that may impact the recovery capabilities of the service provider. Be sure to review the test results and look for improvements.

Infrastructure and platform management

The purpose of infrastructure and platform management is to *"oversee the infrastructure and platforms used by an organisation. When carried out properly, this practice enables the monitoring of technology solutions available to the organisation, including the technology and external service providers."*

This practice includes hardware, software, networks and facilities within its scope; simply put, anything that plays a role in developing, testing, delivering, monitoring, managing and supporting an IT service. The infrastructure and platform management practice covers all phases of the infrastructure lifecycle – from concept to requirements, delivery to support.

Other practices interface with infrastructure and platform management, such as business analysis, architecture

7: Ensuring resilient operations

management, service continuity management, information security management, risk management, etc.

This practice, depending on the organisation's definition, can be applied to the management of the:

- Physical environment
- Physical equipment
- Digital infrastructure

Many organisations will manage infrastructure solutions as services – providing infrastructure to their customers, which are application and/or product teams. If this is the case, ensure the infrastructure and platform teams are involved in the overall service delivery initiatives of the organisation. They will need to follow the ITIL principles (e.g. focus on value, think and work holistically, collaborate and promote visibility) and understand their impact not only on the overall organisation but also the service value system (SVS).

The infrastructure and platform management practice includes two PSFs:

- *"Establishing an infrastructure and platform management approach to meet evolving organisational needs.*
- *Ensuring that the infrastructure and platform solutions meet the organisation's current and anticipated needs."*

7: Ensuring resilient operations

Table 42: Infrastructure and Platform Management PSFs

PSF: Establishing an Infrastructure and Platform Management Approach
Change is the only constant in today's business environment. Technology evolves more and more quickly, creating an environment of continual transformation. Change comes from many different sources, and the infrastructure and platform management practice must ensure the solutions they provide are flexible and scalable in order to support these changes.
To deliver flexible and scalable solutions, infrastructure and platform teams need to have current knowledge and understanding of new technologies and techniques (they need to be prepared for the future!). Evolving technologies allow requests to be fulfilled at a much higher rate, supporting the needs of their customers.
Think about how virtual server farms, single sign-on, cloud platforms, virtualisation, containers and continuous integration/continuous delivery (CI/CD) have impacted the rate (and success) of change and innovation.
To gain these benefits, infrastructure and platform teams need to ensure that the delivered structures support and promote *"experimentation, quick technology adaption, the ability to test theories and hypotheses, change the infrastructure and platform iteratively with feedback, fail fast, and learn from experience and errors in a safe environment"*.
PSF: Ensuring that Solutions meet Anticipated Needs

7: Ensuring resilient operations

To fulfil this PSF, a level of transparency needs to exist between the infrastructure and platform teams and various stakeholder groups. Any solution presented by the infrastructure and platform teams should include both technical and business requirements. Consider these areas as potential sources of requirements:

- Architectural standards and guidelines
- Compliance requirements
- Customer requirements

Standardising the work of and solutions provided by the infrastructure and platform teams is an efficient and effective way to manage current and future solutions.

This includes defining hardware and software versions, configuration settings, management and monitoring tools, and support structures in order to increase the reliability and maintainability of solutions presented.

All designs should be reviewed regularly and validated against current and future needs (e.g. availability, information security, capacity, performance).

Additionally, reviews should also include standard designs. If there are many exceptions to the standard, it may no longer be fit for purpose. Designs may need to be withdrawn or updated to meet current and future strategic needs.

Infrastructure and platform solutions may include third-party solutions and/or components. Review, validation and improvement activities should include these elements, alongside the necessary ITIL practices (e.g. supplier

7: Ensuring resilient operations

management, software and development management, architecture management, service design, and others).

How should infrastructure and platform solutions be reviewed? Consider benchmarking current solutions to compare them with:

- Cloud offerings
- External provider solutions

From a technology perspective, consider automation, consolidation and standardisation to simplify the infrastructure and platforms and also the release resources. All will increase the value proposition of the service provider.

CHAPTER 8: ENSURING CO-CREATED VALUE

This chapter describes the techniques and practices that support the HVIT objective of co-creation of value. The technique that supports the co-creation of value is service experience.

The supporting ITIL practices for this objective include:

- Relationship management
- Service design
- Service desk

We also addressed relationship management in Chapter 5 – make sure you review that content in the context of co-creating value.

Techniques for co-creating value

Co-created value occurs when the consumer benefits from the use of the service provider's products and services, and the service provider also achieves its goals and desired outcomes. The consumer and provider have both fulfilled their needs.

To achieve a return on a digital investment, the consumer's decision-making should be improved because of their access to automated information systems. Just having the information isn't enough though – the consumer must understand how the automated service works so that the information presented is interpreted correctly. Once the decision is made and acted upon, value is realised.

8: Ensuring co-created value

There is a problem though – many consumers don't use information systems effectively. Misinterpreting the data and making poor decisions based on the interpretation creates no value (and can lead to frustration!). Even having resilient, highly capable systems means nothing if they can't be used properly!

Solution? There must be proactive, functional user support. Think in terms of a **value realisation coach** rather than just a service desk.

> Here's a really simple example of value co-creation and missed opportunities. Imagine you use your mobile phone to make phone calls. That's it, that's all you use it for. No text messages, no photos, no Internet browsing, no banking, no games, no apps. Just calls. You're getting some value, but nowhere near the value you could potentially get.
>
> But maybe you don't know all these things exist. Are you, the consumer, at fault? Not necessarily! Your service provider needs to engage with you and provide you with the information you need to get the maximum value. At the same time, you need to share more about what you would like to get from your phone. Co-creation is a two-way relationship.

Co-creation of value means that both the consumer and the provider work together – during and beyond the service

8: Ensuring co-created value

interaction. The consumer needs to be involved with the product or service design and development to ensure that their expectations align with the capabilities of the provider. The technique that focuses on this relationship is 'service experience'.

Service experience

Service experience is a combination of technical functionality and how the output from the service is perceived by the consumer. To achieve a value-driven service experience, the service provider must understand the consumer's requirements and how they match up with their own capabilities. The strength of that connection will determine value co-creation.

When considering service experience, the responsibility for this outcome no longer rests solely with the service provider. The consumer must also 'put skin in the game' by working with the provider to ensure their needs are understood, working with the design and development teams to ensure their needs are properly translated, and then reporting issues, new requirements or improvements in a timely fashion so that value is realised.

This relationship is detailed further in the *ITIL® 4: Drive Stakeholder Value* publication.

Considering the concept of service experience to achieve co-created value, the activities within the service value chain that will most benefit are:

- Plan
- Engage
- Design and transition
- Obtain/build

8: Ensuring co-created value

- Deliver and support
- Improve

Which ITIL practices influence or use service experience? Review table 43, paying close attention to the high-impact practices.

Table 43: Practices for Which Service Experience is Relevant[48]

ITIL management practice	*Activities/resources associated with service experience*	*Impact*
Business analysis	*Understanding user needs and translating them into customer experience or user experience requirements, in addition to traditional requirements regarding utility and warranty.*	*H*
Service catalogue management	*Describing services and offerings in terms of technical as well as experiential aspects.*	*H*
Service design	*Articulating customer experience and user experience needs beyond a basic experience.*	*H*

---

[48] *ITIL® 4: High-velocity IT*, table 4.21. Copyright © AXELOS Limited 2020. Used under permission of AXELOS Limited. All rights reserved.

8: Ensuring co-created value

Service desk	*Being empathetic and having the emotional intelligence to understand users' experiential needs.* *Giving users a choice of communication channels.* *Service experience requires technology and information enablers, such as self-service tools, online portals, mobile applications, call centre tools, and chat.* *Using user satisfaction as a KPI.* *Assessing user experience, while choosing a tool for two-way communication with users.* *Gathering service experience data (rough estimates of users happy/not happy with the service).*	H
Service level management	*Promoting a good understanding of the psychographics of the service consumer and the (emotional) effect of service interactions on the consumer.*	H

8: Ensuring co-created value

Software development and management	The desired service experience informs the design of the user interface.	H
Monitoring and event management	Developing and configuring tools and techniques to monitor service experience and associated events, in addition to technical monitoring and event management.	M
Relationship management	Being empathetic and emotionally intelligent to understand consumers' experiential needs.	M
Service validation and testing	Developing and maintaining tests of the service experience.	M
Supplier management	Engaging and managing suppliers based on both subjective and objective agreements.	M

ITIL practices and ensuring co-created value

The supporting ITIL practices for ensuring co-created value include:

- Service design

8: Ensuring co-created value

- Service desk

Service design

The purpose of service design is *"to design products and services that are fit for purpose and use, and that can be delivered by the organisation and its ecosystem. This includes planning and organizing people, partners and suppliers, information, communication, technology, and practices for new or changed products and services, and the interaction between the organisation and its customers."*

The software development and management practice is quite similar to service design. Let's be clear about their differences as well though:

- **Service design** *ensures* products and services fulfil utility and warranty requirements.
- **Software development** and management focuses on the ***development and management*** of application software to meet utility and warranty needs.

As we explore service design, the activities clearly focus on identifying tasks, defining key information and coordinating implementation. This practice is very much managerial, and it oversees the entire lifecycle of service design. Software development and management would naturally coordinate with service design to ensure a smooth transition of any developed applications to support the new product or service.

Service design has two PSFs:

- *"Establishing and maintaining an effective organisation-wide approach to service design*

8: Ensuring co-created value

- *Ensure that services are fit for purpose and fit for use throughout their lifecycle"*

Table 44: Service Design PSFs

PSF: Establishing and Maintaining and Organisation-wide Approach to Service Design
The focus of the service design practice is to define and agree the approach and model used to design new and changed software and service components. This decision should be made based on the organisational strategy and customer requirements. There should be a holistic view within service design. Consider these possible inputs to the service design practice as part of the holistic approach: - Current service portfolio. - Current and future customers. - Communication and feedback channels. - Ability to innovate and accept change. - Resource constraints. - Risk appetite. - Implementation methods, practices and procedures. - Impact of current and future partners and suppliers. Keeping the previous elements in mind, several different design approaches may be in use in any one organisation. These approaches may differ due to the type of product or service. Regardless of the approach, the design should be flexible and have the capability to adapt to changing circumstances, stakeholders and environment.

8: Ensuring co-created value

Continual improvement is critical for the service design practice. The goal is to discover new ways to meet stakeholder expectations effectively and efficiently, increase customer and user satisfaction, and eliminate waste.

PSF: Ensuring Services Fulfil Fit for Purpose and Fit for Use Requirements

Consider all four dimensions and the part that they will play in the creation of effective service designs. Have you ever seen a service design fail because one of the four dimensions wasn't considered? Ensure a holistic approach is used for service design to guarantee benefit realisation.

Numerous practices will engage in any service design. Clear communication, information flow and early involvement are necessary. The service design practice focuses on identifying tasks, key information and coordination of the design implementation. Additionally, service design will recommend procedures and techniques to use during implementation.

Consider the following practices that would interface with service design – good coordination and communication are necessary:

- Project management
- Change enablement
- Software development and management
- Infrastructure and platform management
- Business analysis
- Service validation and testing

8: Ensuring co-created value

- Release management
- Availability management
- Continuity management
- Capacity and performance management
- Service level management
- Supplier management

Use the Banksbest case study to look at the My Way project from a service design perspective. What elements needs to be considered for each of the four dimensions of service management?

Service desk

Most of us have experienced an interaction with a service desk. As consumers, we come away from that engagement with a positive or negative impression of the organisation. The service desk is often the first and only direct encounter we have with a service provider organisation. The service desk needs to deliver a great user experience and work hard to achieve high levels of customer satisfaction.

The purpose of the service desk is *"to capture demand for incident resolution and service requests. It should also be the entry point and single point of contact for the service provider for all users."* An incident is *"an unplanned*

8: Ensuring co-created value

interruption to a service or reduction in the quality of a service".

The service desk team typically supports multiple service management practices including:

- Incident management
- Service request management
- Problem management
- Service configuration management
- Relationship management

> The service desk can deliver a great experience even when products and services aren't working. What do you expect from a service desk? Think about the lifecycle of an incident – what are your expectations at each stage? How do you prefer to receive support? From a human, or via software? On the phone, or via email or a web form? Why?

Relationships are based on the direct contact and communication the service desk has with users. Any value stream activity that requires user communication will use the service desk.

A critical characteristic of a service desk role is the ability to empathise. **Service empathy** is *"the ability to recognize, understand, predict, and project the interests, needs,*

8: Ensuring co-created value

intentions, and experiences of another party in order to establish, maintain, and improve the service relationship".

Service empathy is a critical element of user satisfaction and the success of the service provider.

The service desk practice includes two PSFs:

- *"Enabling and continually improving effective, efficient, and convenient communications between the service provider and its users."*
- *"Enabling the effective integration of user communications into value streams."*

Table 45: Service Desk Practice PSFs

PSF: Enabling and Continually Improving Communication
Support channels for users should be easy to locate, be easy to use, and provide the necessary support efficiently and effectively. The design of the user interface is determined by numerous factors such as: - Service relationship model and type – is the relationship public or private, internal or external; is the type of relationship basic, cooperative, or a partnership? - User profile – what are their capabilities based on location, age, culture, diversity, etc.? - Service provider profile – what are their technical capabilities, user satisfaction strategy, etc. - External factors – consider the PESTLE model to assess external factors and their impacts.

8: Ensuring co-created value

Due to the advances in technology, communication channels for user support can be provided by a human or through technology. Some examples of communication channels include:

- Human: voice, live chat, email, walk-in; and
- Technology: web portals, interactive voice menus, mobile apps, chatbots.

Typically, service providers will use multiple channels to provide user support. These channels should be connected and integrated or omnichannel.

Omnichannel communication allows the user to start a support call using a mobile application to create an appointment, follow up with a call to a service desk, and then eventually have a solution applied by a technician without ever providing the same information at each progressive check. Multichannel communication that is not integrated could require information to be entered at each step with a risk of creating gaps in the support actions or losing or corrupting information. The need to repeat information can also lead to frustration for the customer.

PSF: Integration of Communication into Value Streams

The service desk provides bi-directional communication between the service provider and the user. The service desk practice focuses on the accuracy of capturing, recording and integrating communication into relevant value streams.

8: Ensuring co-created value

One example of a communication by the service provider to the user would be a notification around planned changes. The content, format and timing of the message is determined by change enablement and release management practices, but the service desk establishes and maintains the communication channel.

User-initiated communication (queries) must be triaged by the service desk, so it is forwarded to the appropriate value stream for action. Once forwarded, that specific value stream processes and acts upon the query following its own specific processes and procedures.

CHAPTER 9: ENSURING ASSURED CONFORMANCE

This chapter describes the techniques and practices that support the HVIT objective of assured conformance. The techniques that support assured conformance are:

- DevOps Audit Defense Toolkit
- DevSecOps
- Peer review

The supporting ITIL practices for this objective include:

- Information security management
- Risk management

Techniques for ensuring assured conformance

Assured conformance focuses on corporate and regulatory compliance for service provision and consumption with respect to governance and risk. HVIT pushes the boundaries of risk-taking, and while taking risks is necessary, internal rules and external regulations must be followed. The assured conformance objective directly communicates to those who are accountable for, or impacted by, governance, risk and compliance (GRC) issues.

A quick reminder: practitioners do not govern; rather, they are governed. Practitioners operate within defined governance boundaries, using their experience and judgement to deal with events. As one's experience and insight mature, knowing when to deviate from the rules because the benefits outweigh the risks becomes an easier decision.

9: Ensuring assured conformance

How is assured conformance measured? Consider these indicators:

- Lack of security breaches.
- Reduced or no regulatory fines.
- No bad publicity.
- No audit issues from either internal or external auditors.
- Reduction in spend to ensure conformance to GRC requirements.

> Many organisations see a conflict between HVIT and conformance. This is absolutely not the case. A growing body of experience shows that ways of working like DevOps can be adopted in some of the most highly regulated and audited industries. I have worked with banks, for example, that are successfully using High-velocity methods to satisfy their consumers and, at the same time, meet their regulatory goals.

DevOps Audit Defense Toolkit

DevOps practices and traditional audit methodologies have a disconnect – the fluidity of DevOps doesn't always match well with the more traditional and hierarchical methods of IT audit.

The DevOps Audit Defense Toolkit creates a link between the DevOps practice and IT audit requirements, clearly

9: Ensuring assured conformance

linking the practice activities with risk mitigation. The techniques within the DevOps Audit Defense Toolkit create a shared understanding between the auditor and the IT function, allowing the auditor to understand the DevOps methodology and be assured that conformance is achieved in the DevOps processes.

For example, 'changes' might be tracked using the CI/CD toolchain instead of being formally logged via a request for change form. The data still exists, just in a different format. It is still easy to recover and audit the necessary information.

When considering the DevOps Audit Defense Toolkit to achieve assured conformance, the activities within the service value chain that will most benefit are:

- Design and transition
- Obtain/build
- Deliver and support
- Improve

Which ITIL practices influence or use the DevOps Audit Defense Toolkit? Review table 46, paying close attention to the high-impact practices.

9: Ensuring assured conformance

Table 46: Practices for Which the DevOps Audit Defense Is Relevant[49]

ITIL management practice	Activities/resources associated with the DevOps Audit Defense Toolkit	Impact
Continual improvement	Auditing provides new information or opportunities for improvement that are formally registered, prioritized, and managed.	H
Information security management	Designing and implementing controls in the product lifecycle to provide extensive traceability and joint accountability.	H
Monitoring and event management	Operational data warehouses consolidating performance and event data provide a rich repository of information to audit implementation and performance of controls.	H
Service configuration management	Standardized configurations to support security and audit requirements.	H

---

[49] *ITIL® 4: High-velocity IT*, table 4.22. Copyright © AXELOS Limited 2020. Used under permission of AXELOS Limited. All rights reserved.

9: Ensuring assured conformance

Knowledge management	*Giving staff and other key stakeholders access to relevant policy documentation and previous audit reports.*	M
Risk management	*Creating a balanced and practical approach between enterprise risk management, technical risk management, and new ways of working.*	M
Workforce and talent management	*Training staff on their obligations and duties to ensure compliance with all relevant policies and regulations.*	M
Business analysis	*Incorporating audit findings and suggested remediation into the product backlog.*	L
Strategy management	*Incorporating regular external or internal audits into a service's roadmap in order to provide independent governance of the service.*	L

DevSecOps

Most organisations have dedicated information security teams that define, manage and improve security and risk-based policies, procedures and controls. In a High-velocity

9: Ensuring assured conformance

organisation, security is now integrated with development and operations.

With this integration, there is a shift in purpose, moving from 'policing' to enablement. Specifically, information security is enabling the development and operations teams to include daily security work in their work, hence the term 'DevSecOps'.

Security-related activities are now embedded in the DevOps activities and the pillars of culture, automation, metrics and sharing (CAMS, or CALMS with the addition of Lean).

Information security is dependent on people's behaviour – those who have been well-trained and follow the security policies and controls can help detect, prevent and correct security incidents.

Traditionally, IT has operated under a 'separation (or segregation) of duties' policy to reduce risk and the possibility of fraud (e.g. release of untested or unapproved code). This can lead to delays, which conflict with the objectives of HVIT. Integrating, rather than separating, duties can maintain the same level of assurance without any negative impact on velocity.

There are many processes and procedures that support information security management. Consider the following activities:

- Security incident management process.
- Risk management process.
- Security control review and audit process.
- Identity and access management process.
- Event detection and correlation.

9: Ensuring assured conformance

- Procedures for penetration testing, vulnerability scanning.
- Procedures for managing security-related changes.

What's the implication of this? If your organisation follows a DevOps or waterfall approach (or any other approach), it's important to understand that practices are not separate entities. Many, if not most, of the activities are shared or they overlap multiple practices, processes and procedures. To create that HVIT environment, information and activities need to be shared and not duplicated. How often have you seen duplicated efforts in your own environment and realised the waste of resources and the impact on the staff and customers?

When including the technique of DevSecOps to achieve assured conformance, the activities within the service value chain that will most benefit are:

- Design and transition
- Obtain/build
- Deliver and support
- Improve

Which ITIL practices influence or use DevSecOps? Review table 47, paying close attention to the high-impact practices.

9: Ensuring assured conformance

Table 47: Practices for Which DevSecOps Is Relevant[50]

ITIL management practice	Activities/resources associated with DevSecOps	Impact
Continual improvement	*Improvements to security controls and policies can be part of the learning and feedback incorporated by development and operations teams.*	H
Information security management	*Designing and implementing controls in a development lifecycle to provide extensive traceability and joint accountability.* *Integrating information security duties into the daily work of practitioners.*	H
Monitoring and event management	*Configuring monitoring tools to continually scan for threats and vulnerabilities so that they can be escalated to the appropriate teams.*	H
Change enablement	*Implementing a preventative control that automatically*	M

---

[50] *ITIL® 4: High-velocity IT*, table 4.23. Copyright © AXELOS Limited 2020. Used under permission of AXELOS Limited. All rights reserved.

9: Ensuring assured conformance

	requires pre-authorization from security management before developers can make certain types of production data edits, including functions that they have entitlements to, based on certain defined criteria.	
Deployment management	Security management provides guidance on key credential management, CD pipeline security checks, container security, automated penetration testing, and data and performance monitoring. Information security management and risk management should be an integral part of the daily work of practitioners.	M
Knowledge management	Giving staff and other key stakeholders access to relevant policy documentation.	M
Risk management	Creating a balanced and practical approach between enterprise risk management, technical risk management, and new ways of working. Identifying and removing dependencies on external	M

9: Ensuring assured conformance

	teams/parties when changing IT services, which may involve delegating approval authority to the team's product/delivery manager.	
	Investing in process automation (e.g. CI/CD) with defined and integrated controls to enforce requirements for the separation of duties. Further to this, employing independent third-party compliance software to suspend the production of deployments until approvals are provided.	
	Detailing the requirements and risk controls in place in supplier contracts to support the integration of duties while adhering to the organisation's security policy.	
	Conducting value stream mapping to identify and minimize process handoffs and approvals.	
Service validation and testing	*Test data management is a key element that helps to ensure continued stability, reliability, availability, and security.*	M

9: Ensuring assured conformance

Strategy management	*Integrating duties to balance regulatory requirements with speed of execution.*	M
Workforce and talent management	*Training and coaching staff and other relevant stakeholders in how to build security into development and operations work.*	M
Business analysis	*Understanding the security policies, standards, risks, potential threats, and vulnerabilities in internal and external environments, and translating them into requirements for development and operations teams.* *Incorporating security requirements into the product backlog.*	L
Infrastructure and platform management	*Security management can enhance infrastructure and platform management (especially when leveraging infrastructure as code) with guidance on secure standards and training, privacy reviews, threat modelling, credential management, and data security.*	L

9: Ensuring assured conformance

	Information security management and risk management should be an integral part of the daily work of practitioners.	
Software development and management	Enhancing software development with guidance on secure coding standards and training, privacy reviews, threat modelling, code analysis, source code and credential management, and data security. Information security management and risk management should be an integral part of the daily work of practitioners.	L

Peer review

The last technique for assured conformance is peer review. Peer review is *"a judgement on a piece of scientific or other professional work by others working in the same area. When applied in software development, a work product is examined by its developer and one or more colleagues in order to evaluate its technical content and quality. This contributes to assured conformance."* Peer reviews have been in practice for years, originating in the engineering industry. The outcomes of peer reviews have shown that it is an effective method of finding defects. In fact, peer reviews have been shown to be more effective than testing.

9: Ensuring assured conformance

Peer reviews promote quality and productivity. Who wants to look bad in front of one's peers? How often has a colleague quickly answered a question you've been puzzling over for hours? The data collected is used to correct defects as well as to evaluate and improve the development process.

Types of peer review can include inspection, a team review, walkthrough, pair programming, peer desk check, pass around, and ad hoc reviews.

> Peer review can be a relatively low-cost, low-impact change that delivers big benefits. Think about where you might adopt peer review in your role and organisation.
>
> Research the different types of peer review (inspection, a team review, walkthrough, pair programming, peer desk check, pass around, and ad hoc reviews) and decide which ones would be the best fit for your organisation.

When including the technique of peer review to achieve assured conformance, the activity within the service value chain that will most benefit is:

- Improve

Which ITIL practices influence or use peer review? Review table 48, paying close attention to the high-impact practices.

9: Ensuring assured conformance

Table 48: Practices for Which Peer Review Is Relevant[51]

ITIL management practice	Activities/resources associated with peer review	Impact
Risk management	Reducing the risk of an unauthorized change being developed and released into production. Cross-checking between identification and assessment of risks.	H
Software development and management	Inspecting development work between peers to increase the quality of code to ensure that it effectively satisfies demand and performance expectations.	H
Change enablement	Colleagues acting as change authorities by performing peer reviews on standard or low-risk changes. Authorizing some changes by peer review or initial assessment of change requests.	M
Continual improvement	Reviewing work done as part of continual improvement	M

---

[51] *ITIL® 4: High-velocity IT*, table 4.25. Copyright © AXELOS Limited 2020. Used under permission of AXELOS Limited. All rights reserved.

9: Ensuring assured conformance

	initiatives, to help increase the quality of the outcomes achieved.	
Infrastructure and platform management	*Inspecting infrastructure and platform components to increase their quality.*	M
Knowledge management	*Reviewing knowledge articles and similar documentation to help eliminate biases and increase the quality of communication across the organisation.*	M
Problem management	*Reviewing workarounds and proposed fixes to errors to increase their quality.*	M
Architecture management	*Conducting walkthroughs of proposed changes to technology architecture to ensure that the changes align with agreed blueprints and roadmaps.*	L

ITIL practices and ensuring assured conformance

The supporting ITIL practices for ensuring assured conformance include:

- Information security management
- Risk management

9: Ensuring assured conformance

Information security management

Information security is a critical aspect in every business (or personal) activity. The impact of data breaches can be catastrophic, and with the growth of digital services, nothing can be more important than the effective protection of IT services and data. The ability to ensure the confidentiality, integrity and availability of data and information is a core competency of any organisation. The purpose of this practice is *"to protect the information needed by the organisation to conduct its business. This includes understanding and managing risks to the confidentiality, integrity, and availability of information, as well as other aspects of information security such as authentication and non-repudiation."*

This practice, along with other practices, ensures that the products and services delivered meet the required level of information security.

- **Confidentiality** is *"the prevention of information being disclosed or made available to unauthorized entities"*.
- **Integrity** is *"an assurance that information is accurate and can only be modified by authorized personnel and activities"*.
- **Availability** is *"a characteristic of information that ensures it is able to be used when needed"*.
- **Authentication** is *"verification that a characteristic or attribute which appears or is claimed to be true, is in fact, true"*.
- **Non-repudiation** is *"providing undeniable proof that an alleged event happened, or an alleged action was performed, and that this event or action was performed

9: Ensuring assured conformance

by a particular entity". This can, for example, include audit trails and logs.

As digital transformation activities continue to expand across today's businesses, the ability to integrate digital services from partners, consumers and other providers securely is paramount. The use of cloud services as well as the amount of data that is being collected, shared and stored has created new vulnerabilities that need to be understood and addressed.

Information is pervasive and will continue to expand. Organisations will need to keep information security at the forefront of all service design efforts and continue to look for new ways to integrate information securely into the services delivered.

> I still see security existing as a silo in many organisations that I work with. It's an excellent idea to have a person (or team) who is responsible for and maintains focus on security, but this shouldn't mean that security is their job alone. It's essential that everyone in the organisation understands how security is a part of their role. This message must be reinforced from induction and onboarding throughout people's time with an organisation. I also see a 'tick box' mentality creeping in – complete this half-hour online course and you can sign off on your security responsibilities for the year. This isn't ideal – leaders need to show they are taking security

9: Ensuring assured conformance

> seriously so that the message then cascades down through the organisation.

The information security management practice includes four PSFs:

- *"Developing and managing information security policies and plans*
- *Mitigating information security risks*
- *Exercising and testing information security management plans*
- *Embedding information security into all aspects of the service value system"*

Table 49: Information Security Management PSFs

PSF: Developing and Managing Information Security Policies and Plans
Organisations need to have clearly defined policies and plans around information security, which need to be disseminated across the organisation and followed. These policies and plans should be measured (to ensure conformance) and reviewed on a regular basis to maintain the viability of security controls. Aspects of an information security policy and plan include: • *"An overall information security management practice approach* • *use and misuse of IT assets* • *access control*

9: Ensuring assured conformance

- *password control*
- *communications and social media*
- *malware protection*
- *information classification*
- *remote access*
- *suppliers' access to an organisation's information and resources*
- *intellectual property*
- *record management and retention*
- *personal data protection*
- *other relevant aspects of information security"*

PSF: Managing Information Security Risks

There are three main activities in the information security management practice:

- **Identification** – using threat and vulnerability assessments, identify all assets within the scope of the SVS and then identify the associated risks to those assets.
- **Analysis** – using the list of identified assets, determine the likelihood and impact of each information security risk.
- **Management of information security risks** – define and manage the controls that prevent or mitigate the identified risks.

Controls are activities or other preventive measures that modify risks. The controls that are put in place are in

9: Ensuring assured conformance

conjunction with other risk-focused practices, such as availability management, capacity and performance management, and service continuity management. Controls are agreed and implemented through additional practices, such as service design, software development and management, infrastructure and platform management, architecture management, service request management, continual improvement, workforce and talent management.

The controls implemented should balance three elements:

- **Prevention** – *"Ensuring that security incidents don't occur"*
- **Detection** – *"Rapidly and reliably detecting incidents that can't be prevented"*
- **Correction** – *"Recovering from incidents after they are detected"*

Finally, controls involve all four dimensions of service management. When choosing a control, ensure it has the necessary effectiveness and efficiency and continually evaluate its effectiveness. Constantly changing environments require ongoing review and improvement of controls to effectively protect data and information assets.

PSF: Exercising and Testing Information Security Management Plans

Plans and policies are critical elements of any management system. If they are not tested, it is unlikely the expected benefit will be achieved. Regular testing is

9: Ensuring assured conformance

needed and will help to train staff in how to recognise and respond to threats.

Regular testing has other benefits as well – faults and/or inefficiencies in the plan(s) can be discovered either during the test or in the review of the test results. Ensure that the various exercises are completed under a variety of conditions in order to provide an element of realism. The higher the impact of a potential security breach, the more often tests should occur.

PSF: Embedding Information Security into the Service Value System

Information security must be embedded in every aspect of the service value system (SVS).

- **Guiding Principles** – all guiding principles should consider the impact of information security, for example:
    o Focus on value – value is realised through an improvement in the quality of information.
    o Collaborate and promote visibility – remember information confidentiality when collaborating
- **Governance** – governance is the backbone of every organisation – large or small. Information security practices need to be embedded throughout the governance activities – ensure the correct attitude towards information security is communicated, define the high-level requirements for information security, and monitor organisational compliance with the requirements.

9: Ensuring assured conformance

- **Service value chain and value streams** – each step of the value stream should reference appropriate information security management practice activities.
- **Practices** – each practice addresses the four dimensions of service management. Each dimension will correlate to one or more information security controls.
- **Continual improvement** – due to increasing threats and dependencies on IT services, providers must continually monitor and improve information security. All improvements, whether or not they have a direct connection to information security, should be assessed for any potential impact.

Risk management

The management of risk is another ongoing activity in service delivery. Risk prevention activities are embedded in several other practices, such as availability management, capacity and performance management, service continuity management and information security management. Even with those activities, there is still a need to formally manage risk. The purpose of the risk management practice is *"…to ensure that the organisation understands and effectively handles risks. Managing risk is essential to ensuring the ongoing sustainability of an organisation and co-creating value for its customers. Risk management is an integral part of all organisational activities and therefore central to the organisation's service value system (SVS)."*

A risk is *"a possible event that could cause harm or loss, or make it more difficult to achieve objectives. Can also be*

9: Ensuring assured conformance

defined as uncertainty of outcome, and can be used in the context of measuring the probability of positive outcomes as well as negative outcomes."

Consider the definition of a service – managing risk on behalf of the customer is an essential part of every service.

When a customer engages a provider, the service they receive removes some risk from them. But additional risks also develop (for example, what happens if the service provider ceases trading?). The service provider should understand and manage those risks. To achieve the value proposition of the service, there must be a balance between the risks removed and the risks imposed by the service. This is the purpose of the risk management practice – to identify and manage risks effectively and efficiently, across all four dimensions of service management.

The risk management practice includes four PSFs:

- *"Establishing governance of risk management*
- *Nurturing a risk management culture and identifying risks*
- *Analyzing and evaluating risks*
- *Treating, monitoring, and reviewing risks."*

Table 50: Risk Management PSFs

PSF: Establish Governance of Risk Management
Governance of risk requires an understanding of two different concepts: • Risk capacity: *"The maximum amount of risk an organisation can tolerate (typically based on damage to reputation, assets, etc.)."*

9: Ensuring assured conformance

- Risk appetite: *"The amount of risk the organisation is willing to accept (should always be less than the risk capacity)."*

Both must be defined by organisational governance. Once defined, practitioners now have an understanding of the boundaries in which they operate. The governance of risk should be discussed regularly at board meetings and risk capacity, risk appetite and strategic risks should be reviewed regularly.

PSF: Nurture a Risk Management Culture and Identify Risks

Once a risk has been identified, it should be documented in a risk register.

There is no easy way to identify risks – perhaps the best way to identify risks is to promote a risk management culture. This means everyone in the organisation should take responsibility for identifying and reporting any risks they discover.

To encourage this behaviour, people need to feel safe to identify and communicate information about mistakes made by themselves or others – without fear of reprisal. Therefore, an effective risk management culture is an open and honest culture.

PSF: Analyze and Evaluate Risks

There are two elements in qualitative risk analysis: impact and likelihood. Use a simple grid and a scale of low, medium and high on both axes. One would plot a specific risk within the grid to come up with an overall risk

9: Ensuring assured conformance

categorisation. For example, a risk that has a high likelihood and a low impact would have an overall risk of 'low'.

Quantitative risk analysis combines the financial impact or other numerical analyses on risk impact. In this case, likelihood is a probability. There are three calculations that can be used:

- **Annual rate of occurrence (ARO):** *"The probability that a specific risk will occur in a single year. It is calculated based on the expectations of how frequent the risk is likely to occur. An event that occurs once every 50 years has an ARO of 2%."*
- **Single loss expectancy (SLE):** *"The expected financial loss due to a risk, each time that a risk occurs. SLE is calculated based on the average cost incurred if the risk happened; typically expressed in financial terms."*
- **Annualized loss expectancy (ALE):** *"The expected financial loss due to a risk, averaged over a one-year period. ALE is calculated by multiplying the single loss expectancy (SLE) by the annual rate of occurrence (ARO). The calculated result can be compared to the cost of controls so an informed decision can be made (e.g., how much to invest in managing a specific risk."*

Quantitative risk analysis is time-consuming, so both types (quantitative and qualitative) are typically used together. A qualitative analysis is performed on each identified risk and a quantitative risk analysis is completed

9: Ensuring assured conformance

on those that exceed a specific threshold (e.g. $10,000) that has been defined in the risk management policy.

PSF: Treat, Monitor, and Review Risks

If a risk is 'accepted', this doesn't mean that no action is taken. Document and communicate accepted risks to the relevant stakeholders and review them regularly to ensure those decisions are still viable.

If the decision is made to manage a risk, develop and implement appropriate controls. Like the information security management controls, they must be maintained, reviewed and improved as needed. Whatever controls are deployed, they must be monitored for compliance and actions taken if they are not being followed. Define appropriate controls across all four dimensions of service management.

CHAPTER 10: EXAM PREPARATION

Here are the key facts about the ITIL 4 Specialist High-velocity IT (HVIT) exam:

- The exam is 90 minutes long. Extra time is allowable if English is not your native language and a translated paper isn't available.
- The exam is closed book – it's just you and your knowledge.
- It has 40 multiple choice questions, and you must get 28 correct, or 70% to pass.
- There is no negative marking (so you don't lose a mark if you get a question wrong).
- There are 13 questions at Bloom's Level 2 and 27 at Bloom's Level 3.

Remember that this course is part of the Managing Professional stream.

Your training provider for ITIL 4 Specialist High-velocity IT will provide you with access to at least one sample exam. When you're ready to attempt the sample paper, try to reproduce, as far as possible, the conditions of the real exam.

Set aside 90 minutes to complete the paper and make sure there are no distractions: don't make a coffee; don't raid the refrigerator; don't check your emails … or Facebook … or Twitter; switch off your phone.

10: Exam preparation

If you don't focus exclusively on the sample exam questions, you will not have a good indication of your possible performance in the live exam. Your sample exam may highlight areas for further study before you take your final exam.

Here are some good practices for taking multiple-choice exams:

Manage your time: if you're stuck on a question, mark it and go back to it later. It's easy to spend too long staring at one question, but there may be easier marks to be picked up further on in the paper.

Have a technique: I like to go through an exam and complete all the questions I feel confident about. That allows me to see how many of the more challenging ones I need to get right to have a successful result.

Trust your instinct: one of the most common bits of exam feedback is candidates who wish they had not changed their answer at the last minute. It's fine to check over what you've done, but be very wary about making changes in those last few seconds.

Use the process of elimination: each question has four possible answers – if you can discount one or two of them then you've dramatically increased your odds of picking the right answer.

10: Exam preparation

Don't panic!: if your mind goes blank, move on, and look at another question – you can do this with online and paper exams. Your subconscious mind will work away even when you're answering a different question.

Read the question carefully: if you're not careful, you will answer the question you **think** you see, not the one that's actually there.

And that's all from me! I hope you've enjoyed the book, and the extra content I've provided along the way will help you to start using ITIL 4 IIVIT concepts in your own role. You can find me on LinkedIn and Twitter; I'd love to hear if you've enjoyed the book and how your studies and your exam help you in your career.

- *www.linkedin.com/in/claireagutter/*
- *https://twitter.com/ClaireAgutter*

APPENDIX A: BANKSBEST CASE STUDY

Company overview

Banksbest was originally HW Banking. It was founded in 1953 in the UK and has branches in most major UK cities. It focuses mainly on business clients, but it also has a mortgage department that offers residential mortgages to aspiring homeowners and buy-to-let mortgages to landlords.

The Banksbest board of directors initiated a digital transformation programme in 2017. At the same time, a new CEO and a new CIO were recruited. A Chief Digital Officer (CDO) role has also been established. As part of the digital transformation programme, the bank rebranded from HW Banking to Banksbest, which was seen as a more customer-focused brand.

Banksbest has defined these strategic goals:

- To be the tenth-largest provider of business banking services in the UK (growing its customer base by approximately 25%).
- To grow its residential mortgage business by 50%.
- To build a reputation as a 'digital first' banking provider.

There is some conflict during board meetings, as the CFO is not fully convinced about the value of the CDO role and the digital transformation programme. She would prefer to focus on cost management.

The head office and data centre for Banksbest are in Manchester. The customer service centre is in Reading. There is also an agreement with a business process

Appendix A: Banksbest case study

outsourcing company in Bulgaria, Employeez on Demand, that provides additional customer service resources during peak times. The customer service centre operates 7 days a week, between 8:00 am and 6:00 pm, and support is also available via the bank's website on a 24/7 basis.

Banksbest's 50 branches are open Monday to Saturday, between 9:00 am and 5:00 pm.

Banksbest has a good reputation in a competitive field. However, the rebrand has confused some customers, and the digital transformation programme has not delivered many measurable results yet. Banksbest needs to improve its online services and embed its new brand in order to grow.

Company structure

Banksbest employs 700 staff. 400 of these work in the bank's branches, 100 in the call centre, and 200 in the head office and support functions. Additional staff are supplied by Employeez on Demand during peak times.

Banksbest is split into divisions:

- Central Operations – provides support services for all departments. Operations includes HR, Finance, Marketing and IT. The IT department has 50 staff.
- Customer Services – this department includes the staff who work in and manage the customer service centre, as well as some technical specialists who work on the systems used in the centre.
- Branches – this department is responsible for the branches providing face-to-face banking services. The branches are expensive to maintain but offer a face-to-face service that some Banksbest customers value.

Appendix A: Banksbest case study

The digital transformation programme is being run by a digital team that operates outside the existing divisions.

Future plans

To achieve its goals, Banksbest and the digital transformation programme team are working on a number of different initiatives. These include the flagship 'My Way' project, which will allow business banking customers to access services however suits them best. Commissioned by the CDO and led by a product owner, My Way will allow business banking customers to use a range of devices to manage their accounts and move seamlessly between branch-based and online transactions. The current plans include:

- Testing biometrics including fingerprint and voice login to support My Way;
- My Deposit My Way, allowing cheques to be paid in using the camera on a mobile phone; and
- Monitoring of customer feedback, levels of demand and which products are most popular.

After three months, the product owner will report back to the CDO. At this point, the project will either be allocated additional funding, will pivot, or will be closed down. My Way is being measured on both governance and compliance and customer satisfaction outcomes.

IT services

All the IT services are run from the head office and the Manchester data centre. Since the digital transformation programme started, more services are cloud hosted by external providers. The main IT services are:

Appendix A: Banksbest case study

Bizbank – the banking system used in the branches and customer service centre. This system contains customer account information and history, including current and savings accounts. Bizbank is hosted in the Manchester data centre, but there are plans to move it to a cloud hosting service to improve its resilience. Bizbank incidents sometimes take a long time to resolve because the original developers have left, and documentation is poor.

Mortbank – the mortgage system used in branches and the customer service centre. As well as tracking existing mortgages, Mortbank has a credit-checking facility that supports mortgage approvals. Mortbank was developed by MortSys, which provides ongoing support and maintenance. MortSys is a small organisation and doesn't always respond within its agreed target times.

Mibank – an online self-service portal being developed as part of the My Way project. Mibank allows customers to check their accounts, move money between accounts, pay bills and receive cheques. The functionality of Mibank will expand as the My Way project progresses.

Banksec – Banksec is an identity-checking utility that is used by Bizbank, Mortbank and Mibank. Banksec uses two-factor authentication, and biometric capabilities are in development.

IT department

The IT department includes 50 staff split into 4 departments, under the CIO:

- Strategic Planning and Business Relationship Management
- Service Management

Appendix A: Banksbest case study

- Development
- Operations (including the Service Desk)

IT has a good reputation generally, but business staff see the IT department as responsible for day-to-day operations and fixing things. The IT department's development role is less well understood. There is also some friction between the digital transformation programme staff and IT staff.

IT service management

Service management does not have a high profile in Banksbest.

The CIO holds a position at board level, and likes to be seen as dynamic and responsive, rather than process driven and bureaucratic. However, some recent service outages have led to a level of interest in service management best practices, as well as assessment of other ways of working including DevOps, Agile and Lean.

There are some culture issues in the IT department, including an 'us and them' attitude that means developers and operations staff don't always work well together.

Sample employee biographies

Lucy Jones	Lucy joined Banksbest as a graduate trainee five years ago. As part of her training, she spent six months in each of the major departments: Central Operations, Branches and Customer Services. During her time in Central Operations, she spent two months in Finance, two months in HR and two months in IT, including working on the Service Desk.

Appendix A: Banksbest case study

	Following completion of her graduate trainee programme, Lucy was offered a job in HR, and worked there for three years. She was then offered a newly created role of Product Owner and is now responsible for the 'My Way' project. Lucy has a good understanding of the Banksbest business units and the IT services that support them.
Doug Range	Doug has worked for Banksbest for 20 years since it was HW Banking. He started work as counter staff in one of the branches and worked his way up to branch manager. His branch was chosen to be one of the pilot locations for the rollout of Bizbank some years ago, and for two years he acted as a super-user for this system, logging the queries he handled on the service desk system. He has recently been promoted to a head office role, including training the customer service centre staff. Doug is working with Lucy on the My Way project, helping to provide customer intelligence, and ensuring the customer service centre staff are kept up to date.

FURTHER READING

IT Governance Publishing (ITGP) is the world's leading publisher for governance and compliance. Our industry-leading pocket guides, books, training resources and toolkits are written by real-world practitioners and thought leaders. They are used globally by audiences of all levels, from students to C-suite executives.

Our high-quality publications cover all IT governance, risk and compliance frameworks and are available in a range of formats. This ensures our customers can access the information they need in the way they need it.

Our other publications about ITIL include:

- *ITIL® 4 Direct, Plan and Improve (DPI) – Your companion to the ITIL 4 Managing Professional and Strategic Leader DPI certification* by Claire Agutter, www.itgovernancepublishing.co.uk/product/itil-4-direct-plan-and-improve-dpi
- *ITIL® 4 Create, Deliver and Support (CDS) – Your companion to the ITIL 4 Managing Professional CDS certification* by Claire Agutter, www.itgovernancepublishing.co.uk/product/itil-4-create-deliver-and-support-cds
- *ITIL® 4 Essentials – Your essential guide for the ITIL 4 Foundation exam and beyond, second edition* by Claire Agutter, www.itgovernancepublishing.co.uk/product/itil-4-

Further reading

essentials-your-essential-guide-for-the-itil-4-foundation-exam-and-beyond-second-edition

For more information on ITGP and branded publishing services, and to view our full list of publications, visit *www.itgovernancepublishing.co.uk*.

To receive regular updates from ITGP, including information on new publications in your area(s) of interest, sign up for our newsletter at *www.itgovernancepublishing.co.uk/topic/newsletter*.

Branded publishing

Through our branded publishing service, you can customise ITGP publications with your company's branding.

Find out more at

www.itgovernancepublishing.co.uk/topic/branded-publishing-services.

Related services

ITGP is part of GRC International Group, which offers a comprehensive range of complementary products and services to help organisations meet their objectives.

For a full range of resources on ITIL visit *www.itgovernance.co.uk/shop/category/itil*.

Training services

The IT Governance training programme is built on our extensive practical experience designing and implementing management systems based on ISO standards, best practice and regulations.

Further reading

Our courses help attendees develop practical skills and comply with contractual and regulatory requirements. They also support career development via recognised qualifications.

Learn more about our training courses in ITIL and view the full course catalogue at *www.itgovernance.co.uk/training*.

Professional services and consultancy

We are a leading global consultancy of IT governance, risk management and compliance solutions. We advise businesses around the world on their most critical issues and present cost-saving and risk-reducing solutions based on international best practice and frameworks.

We offer a wide range of delivery methods to suit all budgets, timescales and preferred project approaches.

Find out how our consultancy services can help your organisation at *www.itgovernance.co.uk/consulting*.

Industry news

Want to stay up to date with the latest developments and resources in the IT governance and compliance market? Subscribe to our Weekly Round-up newsletter and we will send you mobile-friendly emails with fresh news and features about your preferred areas of interest, as well as unmissable offers and free resources to help you successfully start your projects. *www.itgovernance.co.uk/weekly-round-up*.